AUSTENtatious
Crochet

36 Contemporary Designs from the World of Jane Austen

Melissa Horozewski

Photography by Chris Hynes

RUNNING PRESS
PHILADELPHIA · LONDON

DEDICATION

For those who cannot live without books or hooks; to my grandmother Jean, who might possibly be the one person who reads more words than I; and to Lance, Nathan, and Anna—you are the story I treasure most.

© 2011 by Melissa Horozewski
Photography © 2011 by Chris Hynes
Published by Running Press,
A Member of the Perseus Books Group

Books published by Running Press are available at special discounts for bulk purchases in the United States by corporations, institutions, and other organizations. For more information, please contact the Special Markets Department at the Perseus Books Group, 2300 Chestnut Street, Suite 200, Philadelphia, PA 19103, or call (800) 810-4145, ext. 5000, or e-mail special.markets@perseusbooks.com.

ISBN 978-0-7624-4146-4
Library of Congress Control Number: 2011922123

E-book ISBN 978-0-7624-4373-4

9 8 7 6 5 4 3 2
Digit on the right indicates the number of this printing

Book Designed by Corinda Cook
Edited by Cindy De La Hoz
Technical Editing by Susan Huxley
Stitch Charts and Schematics by Melissa Horozewski
Typography: Sabon, Univers, Dearest Script, and Edwardian Script

Photo Shoots:
Production Manager: Melissa Horozewski
Photography: Chris Hynes
Wardrobe Styling: Melissa Horozewski and Hannah Murray
Hairstyling and Makeup: Jennifer Fitzpatrick

Running Press Book Publishers
2300 Chestnut Street
Philadelphia, PA 19103-4371

Visit us on the web!
www.runningpress.com

❧ CONTENTS ❧

"Woman is fine for her own satisfaction alone.

No man will admire her the more, no woman will like her the better for it."

—*Northanger Abbey*

"There is nothing like staying at home for real comfort."

—*Emma*

"Next to being married, a girl likes to be crossed in love a little now and then."

—*Pride and Prejudice*

AUTHOR'S NOTE

It has been my intention to entertain Jane Austen fans with the fictional vignettes establishing each chapter. Though the order in which Miss Austen wrote her novels is widely documented, I found it very amusing to imagine all of Jane's heroines and characters existing together simultaneously. Forgive any anachronisms that may occur as a result of this fiction. And for the most discerning of Janeites, you can find where I made use of Miss Austen's own text where possible in the heroines' dialogue for veracity and amusement.

*I*f you long for the elegance and modishness revealed in the books by your favorite author, Jane Austen, or you are a lover of all things Regency, then this book and these designs were created just for you. *Austentatious Crochet* will have you stepping into the world of Jane Austen and exploring the romance of the Regency era with crochet. Visit with Jane Austen—and expand your wardrobe. Who knows? Perhaps these designs will bring you some romance of your own!

In this book are delightful designs reminiscent of Jane Austen's era, including all the simple adornments and accoutrements so prized in that period of fashion. With thirty-six patterns, designed with both the beginner and advanced crocheter in mind, along with fun facts about Miss Austen and Regency fashion (accompanied with a recipe or two), this book will transport you to Longbourne, Pemberley, Lyme, Bath, or any Austen destination of choice. So if you are a fashion forward chit—that is, a romantic girl who loves Regency-inspired clothing and isn't afraid to wear it with her own twist—then bring out your hooks, brew up some tea, and kick back with this book.

JANE, FASHION,
~ AND NEEDLEWORK ~

Though fashion is not discussed at length in Jane Austen's novels, it was not because clothing and fashion were not of interest to Miss Austen. Jane's own letters, mostly written to her sister Cassandra, included frequent references to clothing, textiles, and accessories. She once devoted more than two hundred words on a detailed description of a "new round gown Mrs. Mussell was making for her," even including her own sketch of the gown in a letter to her sister.

Like today, it can be expected that fashion would be discussed among intimate friends or sisters, more so perhaps as it was quite customary for women of the Regency period to spend a large part of their days making many of their own wearables and accessories. Josephine Ross, in *Jane Austen: A Companion* writes: "Working for young women in Jane Austen's novels meant working with the needle. It was considered undesirable for a female to sit idly about; and in any household—a communal work-basket was generally to hand containing garments to be made up."

Like those of Miss Austen's time, proficiency with a hook and needle today is still quite an accomplishment, more so now in this age of ready-made. I consider the needle arts not only to be a pleasurable and skilled employment of time but a catalyst of further creative inspiration, as did Jane. According to Jane Austen's nephew's *Memoir*, Jane enjoyed needlework immensely and sewed beautifully. He writes that she often interrupted her needlework to jot something down at her desk. She would then return to her sewing only to repeat the behavior, suggesting she knew the connection between stitching and imagination and used the inspiration of such to the fullest. He also notes "some of her merriest talk was over clothes which she and her companions were making, sometimes for themselves and sometimes for the poor."

While Jane Austen died too young to practice what we now know as crochet, (as it was not introduced to England until shortly before her death and not popularized until a few years later, when it was championed by Queen Victoria) Jane is very likely to have practiced tambour crochet. Tambour crochet is a counterpart to an art Jane Austen loved and did proficiently: embroidery. Tambour work was as popular as embroidery during Regency times, perhaps because, like the crochet we know and love today, it was quick to produce. In tambour work, fabric was stretched across a large frame, like that of Mrs. Grant's tambour frame, of which Jane writes in the novel *Mansfield Park*. A sharp hook would then be pushed through the taut fabric, pulling thread up from below to create a chain stitch upon the fabric in a pretty design configuration like that on the tamboured muslin dress Jane mentions in *Northanger Abbey*.

I am immensely pleased at having been invited into a circle of women whose wit, sensibility, and genteelness I aspire to. I have been granted the liberty to extend that invitation to you. We would be ever so delighted if you joined us in crochet, conversation, and cheer.

Note: If you are new to the art of crochet or are just in need of refreshment, I invite you to visit Chapter 7: The Sitting Room (beginning on page 186), before embarking on your first project; there you will find all the essentials you need to begin.

CHAPTER 1

For Your Own Satisfaction: Designs for the Heroine in You

> "Woman is fine for her own satisfaction alone. No man will admire her the more, no woman will like her the better for it. Neatness and fashion are enough for the former, and a something of shabbiness or impropriety will be most endearing to the latter."
>
> —*Northanger Abbey*

"No, no Miss Austen. That simply will not do!" Marianne Dashwo[od] expressed in all earnestness. I watched as she rose from her seat [on] the settee near me. "This is an astonishment bordering upon alarm! Lizzy is off [to] Pemberley. Pemberley!"

"Do sit down," her sister Elinor quietly implored, patting the empty cushion next [to] her, but Marianne continued.

"You are arranging her to meet with Mr. Darcy again. Lizzy cannot," she said e[m]phatically, "be dressed in the brown muslin. It simply will not do."

"Whatever are you talking about, Marianne?" Elizabeth inquired. "Aunt, Uncle, and I are to see the Lakes. That is last you wrote." She spoke, her gaze turning toward Miss Austen for confirmation.

Before Miss Austen could address Elizabeth, Marianne continued. "She has changed it. You travel to Derbyshire, and why would you travel to Derbyshire if not to see Pemberley, and why see Pemberley if not to see Mr. Darcy again?!" Feeling absolutely certain and most triumphant in her aberrant episode of logic, she smiled, looking about to make sure all had heard before sitting.

Miss Austen paused in her stitching and for the first time since Marianne had broached the topic of Pemberley, looked up. "Really Marianne. At times I haven't the faintest idea why I created you with such deep sensibility." Turning to Elizabeth, Miss Austen added, "Plans have changed. You uncle's business will delay the trip by a fortnight. There will not be enough time to travel to the Lakes. You are now off to Derbyshire."

Bewildered, Lizzy set the lace she had been making down and put a hand to her forehead, a sign that a headache was blooming. It was several moments before she inquired, "Am I to see Mr. Darcy then?"

"At the moment I cannot say," said Miss Austen. "I have not written it."

"So there is a chance I might not." Elizabeth queried.

"Please, Lizzy. That level of naiveté is reserved for your sister J-."

Emma was cut short by Anne's skillful interruption designed to thwart yet another war of words so frequent between Emma and Elizabeth. "Well in either case, Miss Austen," began Anne, "I agree with Marianne. If there is the slightest chance she may encounter Mr. Darcy, Elizabeth must be dressed at her best. I have found that when one cannot avoid both the pleasure and pain of seeing a particular gentleman, it always helps to at least be dressed in something that inspires confidence."

"I am quite inclined to agree also," said Emma. "There are few places so elegant as Pemberley and it really would not do for her to be seen in such an old gown. Certainly she must be in possession of something better. Mr. Darcy is a proud man and I am quite certain not inclined to converse with women who tramp around with mud six-inches deep on their dress," she said, glancing pointedly at Lizzy.

Elizabeth opened her mouth to address Emma's affront, only to be allayed once again, this time by Miss Austen. "Well Elizabeth, what is your opinion on your state of dress?"

Elizabeth paused for a moment. How uncharacteristic of her not to be on the ready with words, she thought. Why did the mere mention of Mr. Darcy continue to affect her more than she cared to admit? "While I should not . . . what I mean to say is I am quite certain that . . . well I am not certain how I feel about Mr. Darcy at this present time and therefore I do not know if it should matter or not what I wear." Elizabeth sighed, and then turned toward me. "What would you wear if you were off to Pemberley?"

I smiled at Elizabeth Bennet, for I knew, fellow stitcher, that we had just the thing.

SKILL LEVEL

MATERIALS

Caron *Spa* (25% bamboo, 75% mico-denier acrylic; 251 yds/230 m; dk weight #3 light): #0007 naturally 5 (5, 6, 7, 7, 8) skeins

F-5 (3.75 mm) hk or size needed to obtain correct gauge

Press cloth

Stitcher's Kit (see page 187)

GAUGE

2 fantails (as counted in Row 1, 3, or 5 of st patt rep) and 8 rows (beg with Row 3 or 5 of st patt rep) in fantail st patt = 4" (10 cm) blocked and pressed (see page 16)

FINISHED SIZES

XS (S, M, L, 1X) has circumference of 36 (40, 44, 48, 52)"/91.5 (101.5, 112, 122, 132) cm

STITCH GUIDE

View an online video demonstrating how to create this stitch pattern at: www.stitchscene.com/tutorials

*B*ring a romantic flair to your day by stitching up this elegant, empire-waist sheath. Once you slip into this feminine, sleeveless off-white dress, your Mr. Darcy's heart will skip a beat and an invitation to dine is sure to follow. The fantail stitch makes for a design much simpler to make than first appearances imply and it creates a scalloped hem with no extra work from you. Worked in the round from the top down, you can try it on as you go and make the dress as long or as short as you wish. Create the flattering empire waist so prized during Regency times by crafting the matching monk's cord to tie below the bust. Or put your own modern twist on it with a skinny belt or a colorful slip to wear underneath for a striking contrast. Ironing the silky acrylic yarn beneath a pressing cloth results in a sophisticated finish that will have your acquaintances thinking you are most accomplished.

FANTAIL STITCH PATTERN

See chart page 13.

Foundation ch is multiple of 8 + 2.

Row 1: Sc in 2nd ch from hk, *skip next 3 ch, 9 dc in next ch—fantail made, skip next 3 ch, sc in next ch; rep from * across, turn.

Row 2: Ch 3 (count as dc), dc in first sc, *ch 2, skip next 4 sts, sc in next st, ch 2, skip next 4 sts, (dc, ch 1, dc) in next st; rep from * across ending 2 dc in last sc, turn.

Row 3: Ch 3 (count as dc), 4 dc in first st, *skip next ch-2 sp, sc in next sc, skip next ch-2 sp, 9 dc in next ch-1 sp; rep from * across ending 5 dc in tch, turn.

Row 4: Ch 1 (do not count as st), sc in first dc, *ch 2, (dc, ch 1, dc) in next sc, ch 2, skip next 4 dc, sc in next dc; rep from * across ending sc in tch, turn.

Row 5: Ch 1 (do not count as st), sc in first sc, *skip next ch-2 sp, 9 dc in next ch-1 sp, skip next ch-2 sp, sc in next sc; rep from * across, turn.

Rep Rows 2–5 for st patt.

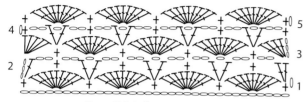

Fantail Stitch Pattern Chart

stitch key
○ = chain (ch)
+ = single crochet (sc)
𝖳 = double crochet (dc)

Notes: Ch 1 and/or sl st(s) at beg of rows do not count as st(s) throughout. Ch 3 at beg of row counts as dc.

FRONT YOKE
FIRST SHOULDER

Ch 26.

Row 1 (RS): Sc in 2nd ch from hk, *skip next 3 ch, 9 dc in next ch—fantail made, skip next 3 ch, sc in next ch; rep from * across, turn. *3 fantails*

Row 2: Ch 3, dc in first sc, *ch 2, skip next 4 dc, sc in next dc, ch 2, (dc, ch 1, dc) in next sc; rep from * across ending 2 dc in last sc, turn.

Row 3: Ch 3, 4 dc in first st—partial fantail made, *skip next ch-2 sp, sc in next sc, skip next ch-2 sp, 9 dc in next ch-1 sp; rep from * across ending 5 dc in tch—partial fantail made, turn.

2 fantails (partial fantails not counted throughout)

Row 4: Ch 1, sc in first dc, *ch 2, (dc, ch 1, dc) in next sc, ch 2, skip next 4 dc, sc in next dc; rep from * across ending last sc in tch, turn.

Row 5: Ch 1, sc in first sc, *skip next ch-2 sp, 9 dc in next ch-1 sp, skip next ch-2 sp, sc in next sc; rep from * across. Fasten off.

OPPOSITE SHOULDER

Rep Rows 1–5 of Front Yoke First Shoulder. Do not fasten off.

BODICE

With WS of Opposite Shoulder facing cont as foll:

Row 1 (joining row): Ch 3, dc in first sc, *ch 2, skip next 4 dc, sc in next dc, ch 2, (dc, ch 1, dc) in next sc; rep from * across ending (dc, ch 1, dc); in last sc do not turn, ch 5 (5, 11, 11, 17)—joining ch made, working in last row of Front Yoke First Shoulder with WS facing, cont as foll: dc in first sc, (ch 1, dc) in same sc; rep from * across ending 2 dc in last sc, turn.

Row 2: Ch 3, 4 dc in first dc, *skip next ch-2 sp, sc in next sc, skip next ch-2 sp, 9 dc in next ch-1 sp; rep from * across, cont established st patt in joining ch (as from * in Row 2 of fantail st patt, see page 12) and ending 5 dc in tch, turn. 6 (6, 7, 7, 8) *fantails*

Row 3: Ch 1, sc in first dc, *ch 2, (dc, ch 1, dc) in next sc, ch 2, skip next 4 dc, sc in next dc; rep from * across ending sc in tch, turn.

Row 4: Ch 1, sc in first sc, *skip next ch-2 sp, 9 dc in next ch-1 sp, skip next ch-2 sp, sc in next sc; rep from * across, turn. 7 (7, 8, 8, 9) *fantails*

Row 5: Ch 4 (count as dc and ch-1), dc in first sc, *ch 2, skip next 4 dc, sc in next dc, ch 2, skip next 4 dc, (dc, ch 1, dc) in next sc; rep from * across ending (dc, ch 1, dc) in last sc, turn.

UNDERARM SHAPING

Row 6: Ch 3, 8 dc in ch-1 sp, *skip next ch-2 sp, sc in next sc, skip next ch-2 sp, 9 dc in next ch-1 sp; rep from * across ending 9 dc in last ch-1 sp, turn. 8 (8, 9, 9, 10) *fantails*

Row 7: Ch 4 (count as dc and ch 1), dc in first st, *ch 2, skip next 4 dc, sc in next dc, ch 2, (dc, ch 1, dc) in next sc; rep from * across, ch 2, skip next 4 dc, sc in next dc, ch 2, (dc, ch 1, dc) in last ch-1 sp, turn.

Next 1 (3, 3, 5, 5) Rows: Rep Rows 6–7 for 0 (1, 1, 2, 2) times; then Row 6 once. 9 (10, 11, 12, 13) *fantails* Fasten off.

BACK YOKES AND BODICE

Rep Front Bodice EXCEPT do not fasten off at end of Underarm Shaping.

BODY FRONT AND BACK

Note: Pm to note beg of rnd being sure to move marker up with each new rnd.

With WS Back Bodice facing cont as foll:

Rnd 1 (joining rnd): Ch 5 (count as dc and ch 2), skip first 4 dc, sc in next dc, ch 2, (dc, ch 1, dc) in next sc, *ch 2, skip next 4 dc, sc in next dc, ch 2, (dc, ch 1, dc) in next sc; rep from * across to last fantail, ch 2, skip next 3 dc, dc in last dc, ch 1—joining ch made, working in last row of Front Bodice with WS facing , dc in first dc, *ch 2, skip next 4 dc, sc in next dc,

ch 2, skip next 4 dc, (dc, ch 1, dc) in next sc; rep from
* across to last fantail, ch 2, skip next 4 dc, sc in next dc,
ch 2, skip next 3 dc, dc in last dc, ch 1, join with sl st in
3rd ch of tch, turn.

Rnd 2: Ch 3, 4 dc in first ch-1 sp, *skip next ch-2 sp, sc in
next sc, skip next ch-2 sp**, 9 dc in next ch-1 sp; rep from
* ending last rep at **, 4 dc in 3rd ch of tch of previous rnd,
turn. 18 (20, 22, 24, 26) *fantails*

Rnd 3: Ch 1, sc in first st, *ch 2, skip next 4 dc, (dc, ch 1,
dc) in next sc, ch 2, skip next 4 dc, sc in next dc; rep from
* around, join with sl st in first sc, turn.

Work even (rep Rnds 2–3) until 30" (76 cm) from under-arm,
ending on even-numbered row. Remove marker.

Fasten off.

FINISHING

Sew shoulder seams. Work 3 rows of evenly spaced sc
around each armhole and neckline. Do not work too tightly.
Check fit over head and around arms; inc or dec sc sts as
necessary. Wet block dress to schematics. When dry, place
press cloth over garment and iron with medium heat to
give work additional shine and drape. Measure under bust,
add 23" (58.5 cm) for tie and make monk's cord (see page
198), or crocheted I-cord (see page 196) to length. Thread
through row underneath bust.

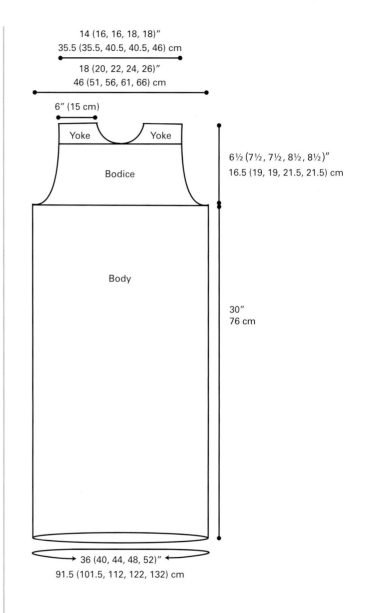

14 (16, 16, 18, 18)"
35.5 (35.5, 40.5, 40.5, 46) cm

18 (20, 22, 24, 26)"
46 (51, 56, 61, 66) cm

6" (15 cm)

Yoke   Yoke

Bodice

6½ (7½, 7½, 8½, 8½)"
16.5 (19, 19, 21.5, 21.5) cm

Body

30"
76 cm

36 (40, 44, 48, 52)"
91.5 (101.5, 112, 122, 132) cm

SKILL LEVEL

MATERIALS

Cascade *Venezia Worsted* (70% merino wool, 30% silk; 218 yds/200 m; dk weight #3 light): #132 tan (MC) 4 skeins; #124 brown (CC1) 2 skeins; #110 ivory (CC2) 1 skein

G-6 (4 mm) hk or size needed to obtain correct gauge

5 La Mode #26293 buttons, ⅝" (16 mm)

⅜" (10 mm) ribbon

⅛" (3 mm) wide elastic

Stitcher's Kit (see page 187)

GAUGE

4 sts and 20 rows in crunch st patt = 4" (10 cm)

FINISHED SIZES

XS (S, M, L, 1X) has bust circumference of 32 (34¼, 36½, 40, 42¼)" /81.5 (87, 93, 101.5,107.5) cm and waist circumference of 28½ (32, 34¼, 37¾, 40)"/72.5 (81.5, 87, 96, 107.5) cm

STITCH GUIDE

View an online video demonstrating how to create this stitch pattern at: www.stitchscene. com/tutorials

*Y*ou won't have to compete for the attention of modern-day Mr. Darcys and Bingleys wearing this top, as the design places you shoulders above the rest. During Regency times, this sophisticated top would have been extended to create an empire waist dress suitable for a splendorous ball, such as the one held at Netherfield. Featuring short sleeves which lay gently at the shoulder, this top is worthy of Austen at her finest. When you wear it, everyone will notice the ribbon and button detailing gracing the lighter color panel along the center for a look that is both extravagant and designed to create an entrance.

CRUNCH STITCH PATTERN

Foundation ch is multiple of 2 + 1.

Row 1: Sc in 2nd ch from hk, sl st in next ch, *sc in next ch, sl st in next ch; rep from * across, turn.

Row 2: Ch 1, sc in first sl st, sl st in next sc, *sc in next sl st, sl st in next sc st; rep from * across, turn.

Rep Row 2 for st patt.

Note: Ch 1 and/or sl st(s) at beg of rows do not count as st(s) throughout.

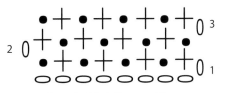

stitch key
○ = chain (ch)
● = slip stitch (sl st)
+ = single crochet (sc)

Crunch Stitch Pattern Chart

LOWER BODY

Note: Worked from Empire Waist to Hem.

With MC, ch 101 (113, 121, 133, 141).

Row 1: Sc in 2nd ch from hk, sl st in next ch, *sc in next ch, sl st in next ch; rep from * across, turn. *100 (112, 120, 132, 140) sts*

Row 2: Ch 1, sc in first sl st, sl st in next sc, *sc in next sl st, sl st in next sc; rep from * across, turn. Pm as foll:

> XS: 25th, 26th, 74th, 75th sts;
>
> S: 28th, 29th, 83rd, 84th sts;
>
> M: 30th, 31st, 89th, 90th sts;
>
> L: 33rd, 34th, 98th, 99th sts.
>
> 1X: 35th, 36th, 104th, 105th sts.

Rows 3–4: Rep Row 2.

Row 5: Ch 1, skip first st—dec made, *sl st in next sc, sc in next sl st; rep from * to first st marker, work next 2 sts of crunch st patt as established (sc, sl st OR sl st, sc—see page 19) in marked st—inc made, move marker to 2nd st of inc just made; cont in established st patt (sl st in sc, sc in sl st) across AT SAME TIME inc in marked sts and leaving last st unworked—dec made. *102 (114, 122, 134, 142) sts*

Rows 6–10: Work in established st patt across, turn.

Row 11: Ch 1, skip first st, work in established st patt across leaving last st unworked, turn. *100 (112, 120, 132, 140) sts*

Rows 12–16: Work in established st patt across, turn.

Rows 17–40: Rep Rows 5–16 twice. *100 (112, 120, 132, 140) sts*

Rows 41–46: Rep Rows 5–10. *102 (114, 122, 134, 142) sts*

Row 47: Rep Row 11. *100 (112, 120, 132, 140) sts*

Next 2 (2, 7, 7, 7): Work in established st patt across, turn.

L, 1X Only

Next Row: Ch 1, work in established st patt (sl st in sc, sc in sl st) * to st marker, inc in marked st as established (see Row 5), cont in established st patt across AT SAME TIME inc in marked sts, turn. *(136, 144 sts)*

Next (4, 9) Rows: Work in established st patt across, turn.

All Sizes

Remove markers. Fasten off.

BODICE

Notes: Pm in tch to note beg of each rnd, being sure to move marker up with each new rnd. Worked from empire waist to shoulders.

Rotate Lower Body so foundation ch is at top. With RS facing, join CC1 to first foundation ch at upper right corner.

Rnd 1: Sc in each st around, join with sl st in first sc, turn. *100 (112, 120, 132, 140) sts*

Fasten off CC1, join MC.

Rnd 2: Ch 1, sc in first st, sl st in next st, *sc in next st, sl st in next st; rep from * around to last 2 sts, sc in next st, sl st in next st, join with sl st in first sc, turn.

Rnd 3: Ch 1, sc in first sl st, sl st in next sc, *sc in next sl st, sl in next sc; rep from * around to last 2 sts, sc in next st, sl st in next st, join with sl st in first st, turn. Pm as foll:

> XS: 25th, 26th, 74th, 75th sts;
>
> S: 28th, 29th, 83rd, 84th sts;
>
> M: 30th, 31st, 89th, 90th sts;
>
> L: 33rd, 34th, 98th, 99th sts.
>
> 1X: 35th, 36th, 104th, 105th sts.

Rnd 4: Work in established st patt (sl st in sc, sc in sl st) to first marker *work next 2 sts of Crunch Stitch Pattern as established (sc, sl st OR sl st, sc—see page 19) in marked st—inc made, move marker to 2nd st of inc just made; cont in st patt as established (sl st in sc, sc in sl st) around AT SAME TIME inc in marked sts, join with sl st in first st, turn. *104 (116, 124, 136, 144) sts*

Rnds 5–9: Work in established st patt around, join with sl st in first st, turn.

Rnd 10: Rep Rnd 4. *108 (120, 128, 140, 148) sts*

Rnds 11–16: Rep Rnd 5.

Rnd 17: Rep Rnd 4 (5, 5, 5, 5). *112 (120, 128, 140, 148) sts* Remove st markers.

Rnds 18–21: Rep Rnd 5.

FRONT

Row 22 (RS, short row): Sl st in first 2 (2, 3, 4, 4) sts—left armhole set up, work in established st patt in next 52 (56, 58, 62, 66) sts, turn—right armhole edge, *58 (62, 67, 74, 78) sts* unworked.

Rows 23–24: Sl st in first 2 sts, work in established st patt across leaving last 2 sts unworked, turn. *44 (48, 50, 54, 58) sts*

XS Only

Rows 25–26: Work in established st patt across, turn.

S, M, L Only

Row 25: Work in established st patt across, turn.

Row 26: Ch 1, skip first st, work in established st patt across leaving last st unworked, turn. *(46, 48, 52) sts*

"I am sorry to tell you that I am getting very extravagant and spending all my money; and what is worse of you, I have been spending yours too . . . I am really very shocking."

—Jane Austen, in a letter to her sister Cassandra

1X Only

Row 25: Ch 1, skip first st, work in established st patt across leaving last st unworked, turn. *(56) sts*

Row 26: Ch 1, skip first st, work in established st patt across leaving last st unworked, turn. *(54) sts*

All Sizes

Rows 27–29: Work in established st patt across, turn.

Row 30: Ch 1, skip first st, work in established st patt across leaving last st unworked, turn. *42 (44, 46, 50, 52) sts*

Next 2 (2, 4, 4, 6) Rows: Work in established st patt across, turn.

Fasten off MC. With WS facing, join CC1 to right front armhole.

RIGHT SHOULDER SHAPING

Next Row (short row): Ch 1, work in established st patt in next 6 (6, 6, 7, 8) sts, turn.

Next Row: Ch 1, skip first st, work in established st patt in next 5 (5, 5, 6, 7) sts, turn.

Next Row: Ch 1, work in established st patt in next 4 (4, 4, 5, 6) sts, turn.

Next 16 (18, 18, 19, 19) Rows: Work even in established st patt. Fasten off.

OPPOSITE SHOULDER SHAPING

With RS facing, join CC1 to outer edge of left front armhole and work as for Right Shoulder Shaping.

BACK

With RS facing and working in Bodice Rnd 21, join yarn in 4th (4th, 6th, 8th, 8th) unworked st from right armhole edge.

Row 22: Ch 1, beg in next st work in established st patt, over next 52 (56, 58, 62, 66) sts, turn—*4 (4, 6, 8, 8) sts* unworked.

Next 8 (8, 10, 10, 12) Rows: Work as for Front to beg of Right Shoulder Shaping. *42 (44, 46, 50, 52) sts*
Fasten off.

FIRST SHOULDER SHAPING

Fasten off MC. With RS facing, join CC1 to back edge of right armhole and work as for Front Right Shoulder Shaping.

OPPOSITE SHOULDER SHAPING

With WS facing, join CC1 to back edge of left armhole and work as for Right Front Shoulder Shaping.

SLEEVE

Make 2

With CC1, ch 45 (49, 53, 57, 63).

Row 1: Sc in 2nd ch from hk, sl st in next ch, *sc in next ch, sl st in next ch; rep from * across, turn. *44 (48, 52, 56, 62) sts*

Row 2: Ch 1, sc in first sl st, sl st in next sc, *sc in next sl st, sl st in next sc; rep from * across, turn.

Next 8 (8, 9, 9, 10) Rows: Work in established st patt across, turn.

Row 11 (11, 12, 12, 13): Sl st in first 2 (2, 3, 4, 4) sts, work in established st patt across leaving last 2 (2, 3, 4, 4) sts unworked, turn. *40 (44, 46, 48, 54) sts*

Next Row: Sl st in first 2 sts, work in established st patt across leaving last 2 sts unworked, turn. *36 (40, 42, 44, 50) sts*

Next Row: Sl st in first 1 (2, 2, 2, 2) st, work in established st patt across leaving last 1 (2, 2, 2, 2) st unworked, turn. *34 (36, 38, 40, 46) sts*

Next Row: Sl st in first 1 (1, 1, 1, 2) st, work in established st patt across leaving last 1 (1, 1, 1, 2) st unworked, turn. *32 (34, 36, 38, 42) sts*

Next 6 (6, 6, 7, 8) Rows: Sl st in first st, work in established st patt across leaving last st unworked, turn. *20 (22, 24, 24, 26 sts)*

Next 2 Rows: Sl st in first 2 sts, work in established st patt across leaving last 2 sts unworked, turn. *12 (14, 16, 16, 18) sts* Fasten off.

FRONT PANEL INSERT

With CC2, ch 25.

Row 1: Sc in 2nd ch from hk, sl st in next ch, *sc in next ch, sl st in next ch; rep from * across, turn. *24 sts*

Row 2: Ch 1, sc in first sl st, sl st in next sc *sc in next sl st, sl st in next sc; rep from * across, turn.

Rows 3–4: Rep Row 2.

Row 5 (dec row): Ch 1, skip 1 st, work in established st patt (sc in sl st, sl st in sc) across leaving last st unworked, turn. *22 sts*

Next 44 (44, 49, 54, 59) Rows: Work in established st patt with dec row (Row 5) every 5th (5th, 6th, 6th, 7th) row for 6 (6, 3, 8, 4) times; then every 4th (4th, 5th, 5th, 6th) row for 3 (3, 6, 1, 5) times. *4 sts* Fasten off.

FINISHING

Steam block (see page 195) crocheted pieces to schematic measurements (see page 25). With CC1, work 1 row sc along inverted V at center front EXCEPT work sl st in center of V for neat angle. Sew RS edges of Front Panel Insert to WS of center front. Sew 5 evenly spaced buttons along panel. Wrap ribbons around buttons and sew to edge of panel beneath the front V row of sc edging. Sew underarm seams and set sleeves into body. The design requires a secure fit along shoulder straps to keep sleeves from slipping. Pin elastic to WS of shoulder straps and create a crochet casing (see page 196) around elastic securing each end of elastic with thread.

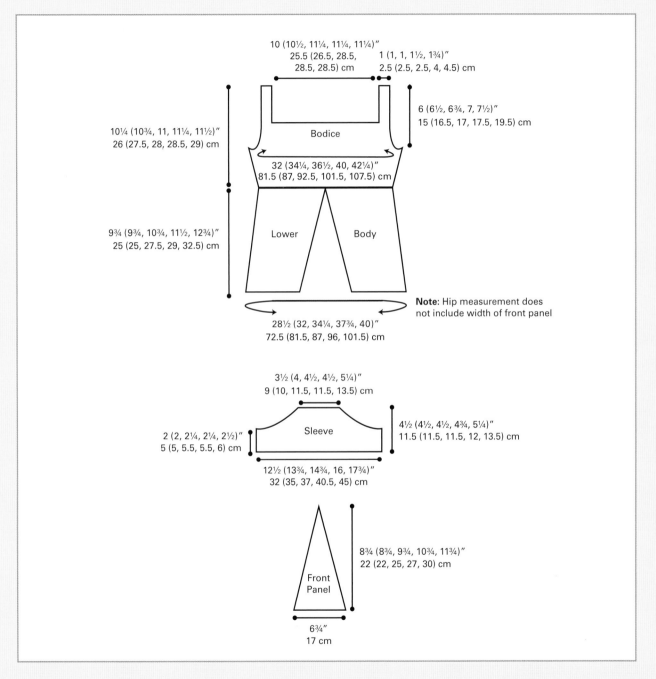

10 (10½, 11¼, 11¼, 11¼)"
25.5 (26.5, 28.5, 28.5, 28.5) cm

1 (1, 1, 1½, 1¾)"
2.5 (2.5, 2.5, 4, 4.5) cm

6 (6½, 6¾, 7, 7½)"
15 (16.5, 17, 17.5, 19.5) cm

Bodice

10¼ (10¾, 11, 11¼, 11½)"
26 (27.5, 28, 28.5, 29) cm

32 (34¼, 36½, 40, 42¼)"
81.5 (87, 92.5, 101.5, 107.5) cm

9¾ (9¾, 10¾, 11½, 12¾)"
25 (25, 27.5, 29, 32.5) cm

Lower   Body

Note: Hip measurement does
not include width of front panel

28½ (32, 34¼, 37¾, 40)"
72.5 (81.5, 87, 96, 101.5) cm

3½ (4, 4½, 4½, 5¼)"
9 (10, 11.5, 11.5, 13.5) cm

Sleeve

4½ (4½, 4½, 4¾, 5¼)"
11.5 (11.5, 11.5, 12, 13.5) cm

2 (2, 2¼, 2¼, 2½)"
5 (5, 5.5, 5.5, 6) cm

12½ (13¾, 14¾, 16, 17¾)"
32 (35, 37, 40.5, 45) cm

8¾ (8¾, 9¾, 10¾, 11¾)"
22 (22, 25, 27, 30) cm

Front
Panel

6¾"
17 cm

SKILL LEVEL

MATERIALS

J&P Coats Royale *Fashion Crochet Size 3* (100% mercerised cotton; 150 yds / 137 m): #226 natural, 1 ball

D-3 (3.25 mm) hk, or size needed to obtain correct gauge

La Mode #26295 button, ⅜" (10 mm)

13 (14, 15) tip-drilled teardrop beads

Stitcher's Kit (see page 187)

GAUGE

3 bobbles and 3 sl sts in Row 1 = 1⅓" (3.5 cm)

FINISHED SIZES

S (M, L) has circumference of 16 (17½, 18¾)" / 40.5 (44.5, 48) cm. Ch-lps have give so finished piece is larger than gauge.

STITCH GUIDE

View an online video demonstrating how to create this stitch pattern at: www.stitchscene.com/tutorials

---

*E*legant chains and petite bobbles trimmed with tiny teardrop pearl beads grace the neck in this stunning necklace. Its flattering drape calls attention to a woman's most delicate area—her collarbone. This distinctive accessory will add drama to any special occasion you have planned. It will certainly catch his eye and quite possibly have you waltzing your way into his heart.

BOBBLE STITCH

Yo and insert hk in next st, yo and draw through lp, yo and draw through first lp on hk, yo and insert hk in same st, yo and draw through lp, yo and draw through all 5 lps on hk, ch 1 to secure.

NECKLACE

Ch 81 (87, 93).

Row 1: Sl st in 9th ch from hk, *bobble in next ch, sl st in next ch; rep from * ending sl st in last ch, turn. *36 (39, 42) bobbles*

Row 2: *Ch 6, skip 3 bobbles, sc in next sl st (between 3rd and 4th bobbles); rep from * across ending sc in last sl st, turn.

Row 3: *Ch 7, bobble in next sc; rep from * across ending ch 7 and sc in last ch, turn.

Row 4: *Ch 8, sc in next bobble; rep from * across ending ch 8 and sc in last ch, turn.

Row 5: *Ch 8, bobble in next sc; rep from * across ending ch 8 and sc in last ch, turn.

Row 6: *Ch 9, sc in next bobble; rep from * across ending ch 9, sc in last ch, turn. Fasten off.

FINISHING

Weave in ends. Ch-lp at beg of row is button loop. Sew button between first and 2nd bobble on opposite end of necklace. Using matching sewing thread and beading needle, sew teardrop bead beneath every sc on last row.

SKILL LEVEL

MATERIALS

Patons *Classic Wool* (100% wool;
223 yds/205 m; worsted weight #4
medium): #77425 woodrose heather
2 skeins

J-10 (6 mm) hk or size needed to obtain
correct gauge

G-6 (4 mm) hk

Stitcher's Kit (see page 187)

GAUGE

12 sts and 9 rows in 5-star marguerite
st patt (see page 30) = 4" (10 cm) with
larger hook

FINISHED SIZE

One size fits most: Depth of 11½",
height of 21" (neck to top of hood),
and neckline circumference of 23"
(29 x 53 x 59.5 cm) when seamed.

STITCH GUIDE

View an online video demonstrating
how to create this stitch pattern
at: www.stitchscene.com/tutorials

*Y*ears from now, you'll tell the story of a woman and her beloved
hood; how its soft fabric always kept her luxuriously warm on the
most cold and dreary of days. Whatever your story, you will benefit from the
classic styling of this tasteful and timeless hood designed to bring romance
to your every day while helping to chase the chill away. Worked in a
five-star stitch pattern (Emma wouldn't have it any other way), once you
master the stitch you can complete this design in just a day.

BS5M STITCH

Ch 3, insert hk in 2nd ch from hk, yo and draw through lp, insert hk in 3rd ch
from the hk, yo and draw through lp, insert hk in first sc, yo and draw through lp,
insert hk in next st, yo and draw through lp, insert hk in next st, yo and draw
through lp, yo and draw through all 6 lps on hk.

S5M STITCH

Insert hk in lp closing Marguerite St just worked, yo and draw through lp, insert
hk in side of same marquerite st, yo and draw through lp, insert hk in bottom
of same st, yo and draw through lp, [insert hk, yo and draw through lp] in each
of next 2 sc, yo and draw through all 6 lps on hk.

5-STAR MARGUERITE STITCH PATTERN

See chart page 30.

Foundation is multiple of 2 + 1.

Row 1: Sc in 2nd ch from hk and in each ch across, turn.

Row 2: BS5M, *ch 1, S5M; rep from * across leaving tch unworked, turn.

Row 3: Ch 1, sc in first S5M by working in lp closing it, *sc in next ch, sc in next

S5M; rep from * across ending sc in lp closing BS5M and in each of next 2 ch of tch, turn.

Rep Rows 2–3 for st patt.

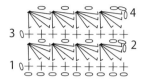

5-Star Marguerite Stitch Pattern Chart

Even-numbered rows are RS
and are read from right to left.

stitch key
o = chain (ch)
+ = single crochet (sc)
⬛ = 5-star marguerite stitch

HOOD

With larger hook, ch 72.

Row 1 (WS): Sc in 2nd ch from hk and in each ch across, turn. *71 sc*

Row 2: BS5M (see page 29), *ch 1, S5M (see page 29); rep from * across leaving tch unworked, turn. *(35 star marguerites)*

Row 3: Ch 1, sc in first S5M, *sc in next ch, sc in next S5M; rep from * across to 16th S5M, 2 sc in 16th S5M—inc made, 2 sc in next ch—inc made *sc in next S5M, sc in next ch; rep from * to 20th S5M, 2 sc in 20th S5M, 2 sc in next ch, sc in each S5M and each ch across ending sc in BS5M and each of next 2 ch of tch, turn. *75 sc*

Row 4: BS5M, *ch 1, S5M; rep from * across leaving tch unworked, turn. *(37 star marguerites)*

Row 5: Ch 1, sc in first S5M, cont in established st patt (sc in next ch, sc in next S5M) across and inc (work 2 sc) in each of 17th, 18th, and 21st S5M and inc (2 sc) in each ch after each selected S5M; work across ending sc in BS5M and in each of next 2 ch of tch, turn. *81 sc*

Row 6 and all RS (Even-Number) Rows up to Row 26: Rep Row 4. *40 star marguerites in Row 6—1 more star marguerite added for every 2 sts inc in previous row; ending 63 star marguerites in Rows 24 and 26.*

Row 7: As Row 5 EXCEPT inc only in 10th, 20th, and 30th S5M and inc in each ch immediately following each selected S5M. *87 sc*

Row 9: As Row 5 EXCEPT inc only in 20th, 22nd, 24th, and 26th S5M and inc in each ch immediately following each selected S5M. *95 sc*

EDGE SHAPING

Row 11: As Row 5 EXCEPT inc only in first, 22nd, 24th, and 26th S5M and inc in each ch immediately following each selected S5M, ending sc in BS5M and 2 sc in each of next 2 ch of tch—multiple inc in tch made, turn. *105 sc*

Row 13: As Row 5 EXCEPT inc only in first and 26th S5M and each ch immediately following each selected S5M, ending with multiple inc in tch—as Row 11. *111 sc*

Row 15: As Row 5 EXCEPT inc only in 25th, 28th, and 31st S5M and in each ch immediately following each selected S5M. *117 sc*

Row 17: As Row 5 EXCEPT inc only in first and 29th S5M and each ch immediately following each selected S5M, ending with multiple inc in tch. *123 sc*

Row 19: Ch 1, sc in first S5M, sc in next ch, cont in established st patt (sc in next ch, sc in next S5M) across ending sc in each of next 2 ch of tch, turn.

Row 21: As Row 5 EXCEPT inc only in 31st S5M and in ch immediately following. *125 sc*

Row 23: Rep Row 21. *127 sc*

Row 25: Rep Row 19.

Row 26: Rep Row 2. (*63 star marguerites*)

Fasten off.

FINISHING

Fold hood in half with right side tog. Seam (see page 200) along foundation ch.

CROCHETED I-CORD

With smaller hk make 75" (1.95 m) long crocheted I-cord (see page 198). Weave I-cord along 6th row of 5-star marguerite stitches from front edge, through center of 5-star marguerite sts and exposing ends of I-cord only on WS of hood.

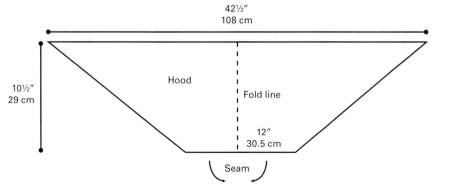

42½"
108 cm

10½"
29 cm

Hood

Fold line

12"
30.5 cm

Seam

"I took the liberty a few days ago of asking your black velvet bonnet to lend me its cawl, which it very readily did, and by which I have been enabled to give a considerable improvement of dignity to cap, which was before too nidgetty to please me. I shall wear it on Thursday, but I hope you will not be offended with me for following your advice as to its ornaments only in part. I still venture to retain the narrow silver round it, put twice round without any bow, and instead of the black military feather shall put in the coquelicot one as being smarter, and besides coquelicot is to be all the fashion this winter. After the ball I shall probably make it entirely black."

—Jane Austen to her sister Cassandra, December 18, 1799

SKILL LEVEL

MATERIALS

Rowan *Kid Classic* (70% lambswool, 26% kid mohair, 4% nylon; 153 yds / 140 m; worsted weight #3 light): #847 cherry red (MC) 10 (11, 12, 13, 14) balls

DMC *Senso* (100% mercerised cotton; 150 yds / 137 m; crochet thread size 3): #1012 black (CC1) 1 ball

F-5 (3.75 mm) hk or size needed to obtain correct gauge

E-4 (3.5 mm) hk

10 La Mode Vintage #1722 buttons, 1" (25 mm)

5 hook and eye closures, size 0

Stitcher's Kit (see page 187)

GAUGE

16 hdc and 12 rows = 4" (10 cm) with larger hk, before felting

FINISHED SIZES

XS (S, M, L, 1X) has bust circumference of 38¼ (40¾, 42¾, 46¾, 50¾)" / 97 (103.5, 105, 119, 129) cm before felting (see page 197), with fronts closed (¼"/ 6 mm overlap). Designed with 5" (13 cm) of wearing ease (see page 189) after felting.

STITCH GUIDE

View an online video demonstrating how to create this stitch pattern at: www.stitchscene.com/tutorials

Make a bold statement with the silhouette of this jacket. Lightly felted to give the appearance of traditional boiled wool, it takes a heroine of courage to make this design. Stitched in a rich red with black corded accents held in place by buttons, the finishing touches on this design are as exquisite as you will be wearing it. Pair it with a crisp white shirt, or even something as casual as a t-shirt, along with jeans and stylish boots, and this cropped jacket is sure to give you the attention you deserve. Authenticate the look even further by using gold buttons imprinted with a coat of arms insignia.

HALF DOUBLE CROCHET DECREASE STITCH (hdc2tog)

[Yarn over, insert hk in next st, yo and draw through lp] 2 times, yo and draw through all 5 lps on hk.

Note: Ch 1 and/or sl st(s) at beg of rows do not count as st(s) throughout this patt.

FRONT

Make 2

With MC and larger hk, ch 33 (35, 37, 41, 46).

Row 1: Hdc in 2nd ch from hk (count as 1 hdc) and each ch across, turn. *32 (34, 36, 40, 44) sts*

Row 2: Ch 1, hdc across, turn.

Rows 3–4: Rep Row 2.

Row 5: Ch 1, 2 hdc in first st—inc made at side seam, hdc in each st across, turn. *33 (35, 37, 41, 45) sts*

Rows 6–7: Rep Row 2.

Row 8: Ch 1, hdc across ending 2 hdc in last st—inc made at side seam, turn. *34 (36, 38, 42, 46) sts*

Rows 9–22: Cont in hdc across, *inc at side seam every 2nd row twice; then every 3rd row once; rep from * once. *40 (42, 44, 48, 52) sts*

Rows 23–24: Work even (Rep Row 2).

ARMHOLE SHAPING

Row 25: Sl st in first 3 sts—dec made, hdc across, turn. *37 (39, 41, 45, 49) sts*

Row 26: Ch 1, hdc across leaving last 3 hdc unworked—dec made, turn. *34 (36, 38, 42, 46) sts*

Row 27–30: Cont in hdc AT SAME TIME dec at side seam 1 (1, 2, 2, 3) st for first row; 1 (1, 1, 2, 2) st for 2nd row; 1 (1, 1, 1, 2) for next 2 rows. *30 (32, 33, 36, 37) sts*

Row 31: Ch 1, skip 1 st, hdc in each st across leaving last 1 (0, 0, 1, 1) st unworked, turn. *28 (31, 32, 34, 35) sts*

NECKLINE SHAPING

Row 32–33: Ch 1, hdc across leaving last st unworked—dec made, turn. *26 (29, 30, 32, 33) sts*

Row 34–36: Sl st in first st—dec made, hdc in each st across, turn. *23 (26, 27, 29, 30) sts*

Next 12 (14, 14, 16, 17) Rows: Cont in hdc AT SAME TIME working 1 dec at neckline every 2nd row for 6 (4, 4, 4, 4) times; every row for 0 (2, 2, 2, 3) times; then every 2nd row for 0 (2, 2, 3, 3) times. *17 (18, 19, 20, 20) sts*

L Only

Next Row: Ch 1, hdc across, turn.

All Sizes

Fasten off.

ANGLED HEM

Rotate work so foundation ch is at top. Join MC to first ch at side seam.

Row 1: Ch 1, hdc across leaving last hdc and ch unworked, turn. *30 (32, 34, 38, 42) hdc*

Row 2: Sl st in 3 sts, hdc across, turn. *27 (29, 31, 35, 39) sts*

Row 3: Ch 1, 2 hdc in first st—inc made at center edge, hdc across leaving last 2 (4, 4, 4, 4) sts unworked—dec made at side seam, turn. *26 (26, 28, 32, 36) sts*

Next 3 Rows: Cont in hdc and dec 3 (3, 3, 3, 4) sts at center edge every row AT SAME TIME inc 1 (1, 1, 1, 0) st at side seam of 3rd row. *18 (18, 20, 24, 24) sts*

Next 3 Rows: Cont in hdc and dec 3 (3, 3, 4, 4) sts at center edge every row AT SAME TIME inc 1 (1, 1, 0, 0) st at side seam of 2nd row. *10 (10, 12, 12, 12) sts*

Next 3 Rows: Cont in hdc, dec 2 (2, 3, 3, 3) sts at center edge once, 2 (2, 3, 3, 3) sts once, and 2 sts once. *4 sts*

BACK

With MC and larger hk, ch 69 (75, 81, 89, 97).

Row 1: Hdc in 2nd ch from hk (count as hdc) and in each ch across, turn. *68 (74, 80, 88, 96) sts*

Rows 2–3: Ch 1, hdc across, turn.

Row 4: Ch 1, hdc2tog (see page 32), hdc across ending hdc2tog in last 2 sts, turn. *66 (72, 78, 86, 94) sts*

Next 6 (6, 9, 9, 9) Rows: Cont in hdc working dec row (rep Row 4) every 3rd row for 2 (2, 3, 3, 3) times. *62 (68, 72, 80, 88) sts*

Next 5 (5, 2, 2, 2) Rows: Rep Row 2.

Next Row (inc row): Ch 1, 2 hdc in first st, hdc across ending 2 hdc in last st, turn. *64 (70, 74, 82, 90) sts*

Next 17 Rows: Cont in hdc working inc row every 3rd row once; every 2nd row for 5 times; then every 4th row once. *78 (84, 88, 96, 104) sts*

Next 2 Rows: Ch 1, hdc across, turn.

ARMHOLE SHAPING

Next 2 Rows (dec row): Sl st in first 3 sts, hdc across leaving last 3 sts unworked, turn. *66 (72, 76, 84, 92) sts*

Next 4 Rows: Cont in hdc AT SAME TIME dec at both edges for armholes as foll: 1 (1, 2, 2, 3) st for first row; 1 (1, 1, 2, 2) st 2nd row; then 1 (1, 1, 1, 2) st for next 2 rows. *58 (64, 66, 72, 74) sts*

Next Row (dec row): Ch 1, sl st in first 0 (1, 1, 2, 2) st, hdc in each st across leaving last 0 (1, 1, 2, 2) st unworked, turn. *58 (62, 64, 68, 70) sts*

Next 1 (1, 1, 2, 2) Row: Sl st in first st, hdc across leaving last st unworked, turn. *56 (60, 62, 64, 66) sts*

Next 2 (2, 2, 1, 1) Rows: Ch 1, hdc across, turn.

Next Row: Sl st in first st, hdc across leaving last st unworked, turn. *54 (58, 60, 62, 64) sts*

Next 11 (13, 13, 15, 15, 16) Rows: Ch 1, hdc across, turn.

FIRST SHOULDER SHAPING

Next Row (short row): Ch 1, hdc in first 21 (22, 23, 24, 24) sts leaving 33 (36, 37, 38, 40) sts unworked, turn.

Next Row: Sl st in first 4 sts, hdc across. *17 (18, 19, 20, 20) sts* Fasten off.

OPPOSITE SHOULDER SHAPING

Join yarn to outer edge of last row of Armhole Shaping and rep First Shoulder Shaping.

Fasten off.

SLEEVE

Make 2

Note: If customizing sleeve length or width, keep in mind felting process will slightly lengthen and tighten sleeve.

With MC and larger hk, ch 35 (37, 39, 39, 41).

Row 1: Hdc in 2nd ch from hk (count as hdc) and in each ch across, turn. *34 (36, 38, 38, 40) sts*

Next 3 (3, 3, 1, 1) Rows: Ch 1, hdc across, turn.

Next Row: Ch 1, 2 hdc in first st, hdc across ending 2 hdc in last st, turn. *36 (38, 40, 40, 42) sts*

Next 45 (45, 45, 48, 49) Rows: Cont in hdc working inc at both edges every 5th (5th, 5th, 4th, 4th) row for 9 (9, 9, 12, 5) times; every 3rd row for 0 (0, 0, 0, 7) times; then every 4th row for 0 (0, 0, 0, 2) times. *54 (56, 58, 64, 70) sts*

Next 3 (3, 3, 0, 0) Rows: Ch 1, hdc across, turn.

CAP SHAPING

Next 2 Rows: Sl st in first 3 sts, hdc across leaving last 3 sts unworked, turn. *42 (44, 46, 52, 58) sts*

Next Row: Sl st in first 2 (2, 2, 2, 3) sts, hdc across leaving last 2 (2, 2, 2, 3) sts unworked, turn. *38 (40, 42, 48, 52) sts*

Next Row: Sl st in first 1 (1, 2, 2, 2) st, hdc across leaving last 1 (1, 2, 2, 2) st unworked, turn. *36 (38, 38, 44, 48) sts*

Next Row: Sl st in first 1 (1, 1, 1, 2) st, hdc across leaving last 1 (1, 1, 1, 2) st unworked, turn. *34 (36, 36, 42, 44) sts*

Next Row: Ch 1, hdc across, turn.

Next 7 (8, 9, 11, 11) Rows: Sl st in first st, hdc across leaving last st unworked, turn. *20 (20, 20, 20, 22) sts.*

S, M, L, 1X Only

Next Row: Ch 1, hdc across, turn.

All Sizes

Next Row: Sl st in first 2 sts, hdc across leaving last 2 sts unworked. *16 (16, 16, 16, 18) sts*
Fasten off.

FINISHING

Sew shoulder and underarm seams. Set in sleeves. Sew side seams. With MC and larger hk, work 1 row evenly spaced sl sts around hem.
Fasten off.

COLLAR

With MC and larger hk, work 5 rows hdc around neck from Left Front edge to Right Front edge. Finish with 1 row of sl sts down front side of collar to neckline edge on each side. Check fit; once felted, stitches cannot be reworked.

FELTING

Lightly felt (see page 197), checking often to ensure garment does not shrink too much. Remove when stitch definition is vaguely discernable. While felting, do not leave garment unattended as felted stitches cannot be stretched to size. Remove from washing machine and block as close to schematic measurements as possible.

BUTTON PLACEMENT

Customize button placement and band lengths to bust height. As shown, beginning at 1½" (4 cm) above hem at front edge center buttons are 3" (7.5 cm) apart vertically. The first two sets of buttons are spaced 4½" (11.5 cm) apart horizontally, the third set 7" (18 cm) apart, the fourth set 9" (23 cm), and the fifth set 10" (25.5 cm). Sew on buttons.

Note: If altering horizontal distance between set of buttons, adjust number of rows in Button Band to match. Button Bands must stretch tautly across fronts when garment is closed.

BUTTON BANDS
ONE AND TWO

With CC1 and smaller hk, ch 11, join with sl st in first ch—button loop made.

Rnd 1: Ch 2—picot ridge made, 2 sc in loop, ch 2, turn. (Take a moment to see whether your gauge is correct by slipping lp around button on jacket. If too tight, work more chs before forming a ring, too loose, work less.)

Row 2: Sc in 2 sc, ch 2, turn.

Rows 3–11: Rep Row 2.

Row 12: Ch 8, skip sc, sl st in next sc—button loop made.
Fasten off.

BANDS THREE,
FOUR, AND FIVE

Rep as for Band 1 working 9 additional rows for Band 3, 15 for band 4, and 18 for band 5 before making 2nd loop. Starch bands. Secure around buttons. Sew hook and eye closures on WS of jacket fronts beneath each band.

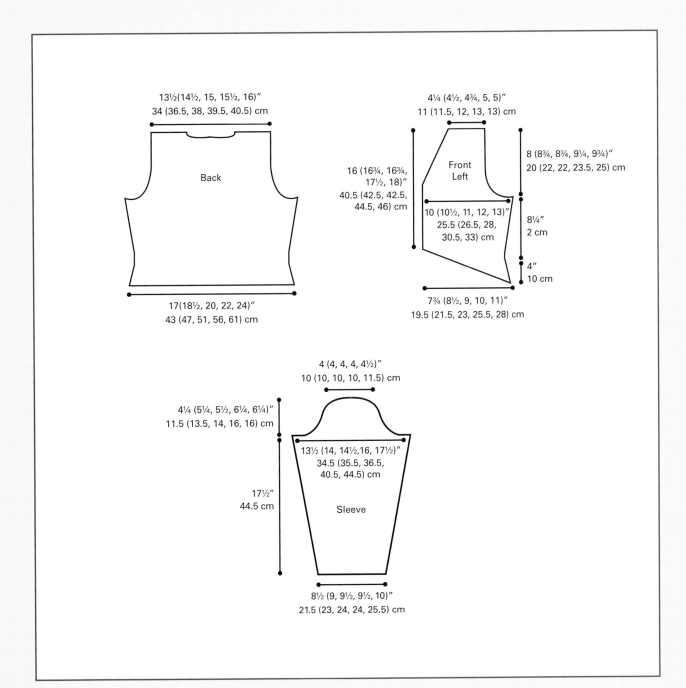

13½(14½, 15, 15½, 16)"
34 (36.5, 38, 39.5, 40.5) cm

Back

17(18½, 20, 22, 24)"
43 (47, 51, 56, 61) cm

4¼ (4½, 4¾, 5, 5)"
11 (11.5, 12, 13, 13) cm

Front
Left

16 (16¾, 16¾, 17½, 18)"
40.5 (42.5, 42.5, 44.5, 46) cm

8 (8¾, 8¾, 9¼, 9¾)"
20 (22, 22, 23.5, 25) cm

10 (10½, 11, 12, 13)"
25.5 (26.5, 28, 30.5, 33) cm

8¼"
2 cm

4"
10 cm

7¾ (8½, 9, 10, 11)"
19.5 (21.5, 23, 25.5, 28) cm

4 (4, 4, 4, 4½)"
10 (10, 10, 10, 11.5) cm

4¼ (5¼, 5½, 6¼, 6¼)"
11.5 (13.5, 14, 16, 16) cm

13½ (14, 14½,16, 17½)"
34.5 (35.5, 36.5, 40.5, 44.5) cm

17½"
44.5 cm

Sleeve

8½ (9, 9½, 9½, 10)"
21.5 (23, 24, 24, 25.5) cm

SKILL LEVEL

MATERIALS

Knit Picks *Gloss* (70% merino wool, 30% silk; 220 yds / 201 m; fingering weight #1 superfine): kenai 8 (8, 9, 10, 11, 12) skeins

E-4 (3.5 mm) hk or size needed to obtain correct gauge

⅜" (10 mm) ribbon, length to fit bust measurement plus 23" (58.5 cm)

Silk rose

Stitcher's Kit (see page 187)

GAUGE

6 shells and 12 rows in begonia st patt = 4" (10 cm)

FINISHED SIZES

XS (S, M, L, 1X, 2X) has bust circumference of 32½ (35, 39, 41½, 44½, 49½)"/ 82.5 (89, 99, 105.5, 113, 126) cm

STITCH GUIDE

View an online video demonstrating how to create this stitch pattern at: www.stitchscene.com/tutorials

*M*ove beautifully and effortlessly through your day in this simply shaped, jewel-tone sweater. Composed in a delightful stitch with a superfine yarn, the drape is flattering and the design is as comfortable as the day is long. The waist is simply shaped using ribbon with added accoutrements to create a gathered empire waist. A very forgiving garment for all figures. Further style the sweater to suit your mood by weaving through metallic ribbon or a skinny belt. Just pin up your tresses and slip into a pair of skimmers for a demure glamour that will awaken your beau's interest right away.

BEGONIA STITCH PATTERN

Foundation ch is multiple of 3 + 3.

Row 1: (Sc, ch 1, sc) in 3rd ch from hk—shell made, *skip 2 ch, (sc, ch 1, sc) in next ch; rep from * across, turn.

Row 2: Ch 1, (sc, ch 1, sc) in each ch-sp across, turn.

Rep Row 2 for st patt.

Note: Ch 1 and/or sl st(s) at beg of rows do not count as st(s) throughout.

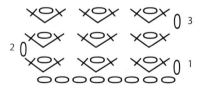

Begonia Stitch Pattern Chart

stitch key
○ = chain (ch)
+ = single crochet (sc)

FRONT

Ch 75 (81, 90, 96, 102, 114).

Row 1: (Sc, ch 1, sc) in 3rd ch from hk—shell made, *skip 2 ch, (sc, ch 1, sc) in next ch; rep from * across, turn. *25 (27, 30, 32, 34, 38) shells*

Row 2: Ch 1, (sc, ch 1, sc) in each ch-sp across, turn.

Next 32 (34, 36, 36, 36, 36) Rows: Rep Row 2.

Next Row (mesh for ribbon): Ch 4, (dc, ch 1) in each ch-sp across, dc in last sc, turn. *26 (28, 31, 33, 35, 39) ch-sps*

Next Row: Ch 1, skip first dc, *(sc, ch 1, sc) in next dc; rep from * across leaving tch unworked, turn. *25 (27, 30, 32, 34, 38) shells*

Next 9 Rows: Rep Row 2.

ARMHOLE SHAPING

Next Row (dec row): Sl st in first 0 (0, 0, 0, 0, 3) sts, sc in first (first, first, first, first, next) ch-sp, *(sc, ch 1, sc) in next ch-sp; rep from * across to last 1 (1, 1, 1, 1, 2) shell, sc in ch-sp, turn. *23 (25, 28, 30, 32, 34) shells*

XS Only

Row 47: Ch 1, (sc, ch 1, sc) in each ch-sp; across leaving last sc unworked, turn.

All Sizes

Next 1 (2, 3, 3, 3, 4) Row: Ch 1, sc in first ch-sp, *(sc, ch 1, sc) in next ch-sp; rep from * across ending sc in last ch-sp and leaving last sc unworked, turn. *21 (21, 22, 24, 26, 26) shells*

Next 10 (12, 14, 5, 5, 4) Rows: Ch 1, (sc, ch 1, sc) in each ch-sp across, turn.

L, 1X, 2X Only

Next Row: Ch 1, sc in first ch-sp, *(sc, ch 1, sc) in next ch-sp; rep from * across ending sc in last ch-sp, turn. *(22, 24, 24) shells*

Next Row: Ch 1, (sc, ch 1, sc) in each ch-sp across leaving last sc unworked, turn.

Next (8, 14, 16) Rows: Ch 1, (sc, ch 1, sc) in each ch-sp across, turn.

All Sizes

Cont with Neckline Shaping.

FIRST NECKLINE SHAPING

Next Row (short row): Ch 1, (sc, ch 1, sc) in first 10 (10, 11, 11, 12, 12) ch-sps, turn—11 (11, 11, 11, 12, 12) shells unworked.

Next Row (dec row): Ch 1, sc in first ch-sp, (sc, ch 1, sc) in next ch-sp; rep from * across, turn. *9 (9, 10, 10, 11, 11) shells*

Next Row (dec row): Ch 1, (sc, ch 1, sc) in each ch-sp across to last ch-sp, sc in last ch-sp leaving last sc unworked, turn. *8 (8, 9, 9, 10, 10) shells*

Next 4 Rows: Work in established st patt AT SAME TIME dec 1 ch-sp at neckline every 2nd row (sc in first ch-sp of row

---

"My gown is to be trimmed everywhere with white ribbon plaited on, somehow or other. Ribbon trimmings are all the fashion at Bath . . . now I am trying to draw it up into kind of roses, instead of putting it in plain double plaits."

—Jane Austen in letters

OR leaving last shell unworked at end of row). *6 (6, 7, 7, 8, 8) shells*

Next 3 Rows: Work in established st patt AT SAME TIME dec 1 ch-sp at neckline every row. *3 (3, 4, 4, 5, 5) shells*

Fasten off.

OPPOSITE NECKLINE SHAPING

Join yarn to unworked edge of last row of Armhole Shaping and rep First Neckline Shaping.

BACK

Work as for Front to Neckline Shaping.

Next 6 Rows: Ch 1, (sc, ch 1, sc) in each ch-sp across, turn. *21 (21, 22, 22, 24, 24) shells*

FIRST SHOULDER SHAPING

Next Row (short row): Ch 1, (sc, ch 1, sc) in first 6 (6, 7, 7, 8, 8) ch-sps leaving 15 (15, 15, 15, 16, 16) ch-sps unworked, turn.

Next Row: Ch 1, sc in first ch-sp *(sc, ch 1, sc) in next ch-sp; rep from * across, turn. *5 (5, 6, 6, 7, 7) shells*

Next Row: Ch 1, (sc, ch 1, sc) in each ch-sp across to last ch-sp, sc in last ch-sp leaving last sc unworked, turn. *4 (4, 5, 5, 6, 6) shells.*

Next Row: Ch 1, sc in first ch-sp *(sc, ch 1, sc) in next ch-sp; rep from * across, turn. *3 (3, 4, 4, 5, 5) shells*

All Sizes

Fasten off.

OPPOSITE SHOULDER SHAPING

Join yarn to opposite edge and rep First Shoulder Shaping.

SLEEVE

Make 2

Ch 42 (42, 48, 48, 54, 54).

Row 1: (Sc, ch 1, sc) in 3rd ch from hk, *skip 2 chs, (sc, ch 1, sc) in next ch; rep from * across ending (sc, ch 1, sc) in last ch, turn. *14 (14, 16, 16, 18, 18) shells*

Row 2: Ch 1, (sc, ch 1, sc) in each ch-sp across, turn.

XS, M Only

Rows 3–14: Rep Row 2.

Row 15: Ch 1, (sc, ch 1, sc, ch 1, sc) in first ch-sp, *(sc, ch 1, sc) in next ch-sp; rep from * across ending (sc, ch 1, sc, ch 1, sc) in last ch-sp, turn. *16 (18) shells*

Rows 16–45: Rep Rows 1–15 twice. *20 (22) shells*

Rows 46–53: Rep Row 2.

S, L, 1X, 2X Only

Next 5 Rows: Rep Row 2.

Next Row (inc row): Ch 1, (sc, ch, sc, ch, sc) in first ch-sp, *(sc, ch, sc) in next ch-sp; rep from * across ending (sc, ch, sc, ch, sc) in last ch-sp, turn. *(16, 18, 20, 20) shells*

Rows 9–53: Cont in established st patt working inc row every (15, 13, 11, 8) rows for (3, 3, 5, 6) times, turn. *(22, 24, 30, 32) shells*

All Sizes

Cont with Cap Shaping.

CAP SHAPING

Row 54: Sl st in first 0 (0, 0, 0, 0, 3) sts, sc in first (first, first, first, first, next) ch-sp, *(sc, ch 1, sc) in next ch-sp; rep from * across to last 1 (1, 1, 1, 1, 2) shell, sc in next ch-sp leaving 0 (0, 0, 0, 0, 1) ch-sp unworked, turn. *18 (20, 20, 22, 28, 28) shells*

Ladies often upcycled their clothing during Regency times by adding trimming, such as lace, to give new life to a dress or bonnet, inserting a flounce or two to update the style, or dyeing a garment in the season's most popular color to freshen it up. If the garment was beyond help, it was often repurposed into other items, such as an older muslin dress into handkerchiefs that could then be embroidered.

XS Only

Row 55: Ch 1, *(sc, ch 1, sc) in first ch-sp; rep from * across, turn.

All Sizes

Next 1 (2, 2, 3, 3, 3) Row (dec row): Ch 1, sc in first ch-sp, *(sc, ch 1, sc) in next ch-sp; rep from * across ending sc in last ch-sp, turn. *16 (16, 16, 16, 22, 22) shells*

Next 9 (9, 10, 12, 18, 18) Rows: Cont in established st patt with dec row every 3rd row 3 (3, 2, 0, 6, 6) times; then every 4th row 0 (0, 1, 3, 0, 0) times. *10 shells*

L Only

Next Row: Ch 1, *(sc, ch 1, sc) in first ch-sp; rep from * across, turn.

FINISHING

Steam block to schematic measurements. With RS tog and taking care to line up rows, sew shoulder and underarm seams, set in sleeves, and sew side seams. Draw ribbon through mesh row. Attach silk rose.

EDGING

With RS facing, join yarn to any st at hemline, ch 1, *sc, skip 1 st, 5 dc in next st, skip 1 st; rep from * evenly spaced around, join with sl st in ch 1. Fasten off. Weave in ends. Rep for neckline and cuffs.

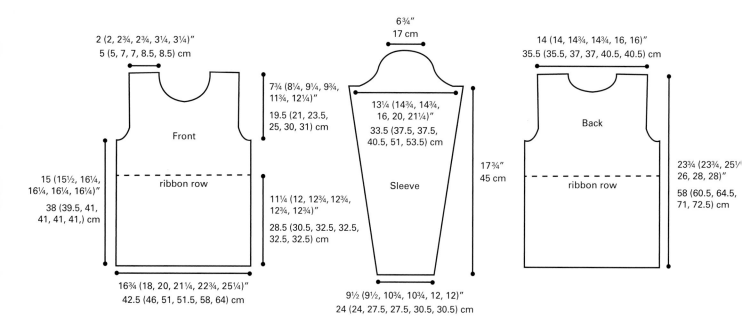

Front

2 (2, 2¾, 2¾, 3¼, 3¼)"
5 (5, 7, 7, 8.5, 8.5) cm

7¾ (8¼, 9¼, 9¾, 11¾, 12¼)"
19.5 (21, 23.5, 25, 30, 31) cm

ribbon row

15 (15½, 16¼, 16¼, 16¼, 16¼)"
38 (39.5, 41, 41, 41,) cm

16¾ (18, 20, 21¼, 22¾, 25¼)"
42.5 (46, 51, 51.5, 58, 64) cm

Sleeve

6¾"
17 cm

13¼ (14¾, 14¾, 16, 20, 21¼)"
33.5 (37.5, 37.5, 40.5, 51, 53.5) cm

17¾"
45 cm

11¼ (12, 12¾, 12¾, 12¾, 12¾)"
28.5 (30.5, 32.5, 32.5, 32.5, 32.5) cm

9½ (9½, 10¾, 10¾, 12, 12)"
24 (24, 27.5, 27.5, 30.5, 30.5) cm

Back

14 (14, 14¾, 14¾, 16, 16)"
35.5 (35.5, 37, 37, 40.5, 40.5) cm

ribbon row

23¾ (23¾, 25½ 26, 28, 28)"
58 (60.5, 64.5, 71, 72.5) cm

❧ REGENCY HAT ☙

SKILL LEVEL

MATERIALS

Bernat *Alpaca* (70% acrylic, 30% alpaca; 120 yds/
110 m; chunky weight #5 bulky): #93531 tomato
(MC) 3 skeins

Patons *Classic Wool* (100% wool; 223 yds/205 m;
worsted weight #4 medium): small amount each
of #00225 dark grey mix (CC1); #77425 woodrose
heather (CC2); #77208 jade heather (CC3)

G-6 (4 mm) hk

E-4 (3.5 mm) hk or size needed to obtain correct
gauge

Glue

1" (2.5 cm) pin backing

Stitcher's Kit (see page 187)

GAUGE

16 sc and 9 rows or 7 rnds = 4" (10 cm) with smaller
hk

FINISHED SIZES

One size fits most: Band will expand to fit circumference of 17–22 (43–56 cm) when worn.

STITCH GUIDE

View an online video demonstrating how to create
this stitch pattern at: www.stitchscene.com/tutorials

This cap, inspired by the classic Regency bonnet, is a modern take on a period design. The wider-style brim protects your delicate skin while allowing you to play the coquette with ease. Featuring vintage colors and a perfectly positioned flower brooch as a finishing touch, follow Jane's advice and make yourself a hat or two to save yourself a "world of torment in hairdressing."

SINGLE CROCHET DECREASE STITCH (sc2tog)

Insert hk in st, yo and draw through st, insert hk in next st, yo and draw through st, yo and draw through all 3 lps on hk.

FRONT POST SINGLE CROCHET STITCH (fpsc)

Insert hk from front to back around post of specified stitch in previous row, work as for single crochet.

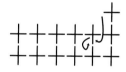

Front post single crochet stitch

TAMBOUR CROCHET STITCHING

Start chain on crocheted fabric surface with yarn beneath finished work at beg of desired design line. Insert hk through fabric, yo and draw through lp. *Working along design line, insert hk through crocheted fabric slightly forward from last position, yo and draw lp through fabric and through lp on hk—surface ch made. Rep from * along design line. At end of line cut working yarn, remove hk from last lp, place hk underneath fabric and draw through lp. Draw yarn tail through lp to fasten off on WS.

CROWN

Notes: Working to gauge is most important for shaping this hat. Bulky yarn is worked on small hk to create tight stitches stiff enough to hold desired shape. Small hk tends to split plies of thick yarn so take care when working yo and drawing yarn through.

With MC and smaller hk, ch 2, join with sl st in first ch.

Rnd 1: 6 sc in 2nd ch from hk. Pm in first st to note beg of rnd being sure to move marker up with each new rnd.

Rnd 2: 2 sc in each sc around. *12 sts*

Rnd 3: *Sc in next sc, 2 sc in next sc—inc made; rep from * around. *18 sts*

Rnd 4: *Sc in next 2 sc, 2 sc in next sc; rep from * around. *24 sts*

Rnd 5: *Sc in next 3 sc, 2 sc in next sc; rep from * around. *30 sts*

Next 14 Rnds: Sc around AT SAME TIME, as already established, for each new rnd work even for 1 more st before working inc. *114 sts*

Rnd 20: *Sc in each of next 17 sc, sc2tog—dec made, see page 47; rep from * around. *108 sts*

Rnd 21: *Sc in each of next 16 sc, sc2tog; rep from * around. *102 sts*

Next 6 Rnds: Sc around AT SAME TIME, as already established, for each new rnd work even for 1 less st before working dec. *66 sts*

BAND

Rnd 28: Fpsc (see page 47) in each of next 40 sts, sc in each of next 26 sts.

Rnd 29: Sc in first 18 sts, 2 sc in next sc, sc in next sc, 2 sc in next sc, sc around. *68 sts*

Rnd 30: Sc in next 19 sc, 2 sc in next sc, sc in next sc, 2 sc in next sc, sc around. *70 sts*

BRIM SHAPING

Note: Ch 1 at beg of row does not count as st.

Row 31 (short row): Sc in next 20 sc, 2 sc in next sc, sc in next sc, 2 sc in next sc, sc in next 21 sts leaving 26 sts unworked, turn. *46 sts*

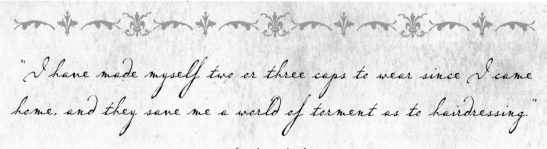

"I have made myself two or three caps to wear since I came home, and they save me a world of torment as to hairdressing."

—Jane Austen, in a letter

Rows 32-37: Ch 1, sc across, turn.

Row 38: Ch 1, sc2tog, sc across to last 2 sts, sc2tog, turn. *44 sts*

Row 39: Ch 1, sc2tog, *sc in next 4 sts, sc2tog; rep from * across, turn. *36 sts*

Row 40: Ch 1, sc2tog, sc in next 2 sts, sc2tog *sc in next 4 sts, sc2tog; rep from * across, turn. *29 sts*

Row 41: Ch 1, sc2tog, *sc in next 7 sts, sc2tog; rep from * across. *25 sts*

Fasten off. Weave in ends.

FLOWER BROOCH

With CC1 and larger hk, ch 2.

Rnd 1: 6 sc in 2nd ch from hk.

Rnd 2: 2 sc in each sc around. *12 sts*

PETALS

Rnd 3: With CC2, ch 2, skip first st *sc in next st, ch 2, skip next st; rep from * around, join with sl st in joining sl st of rnd 1 (6 ch-lps).

Rnd 3: (Sl st, ch 2, 3 dc, ch 2, sl st) in each ch-lp around. Fasten off.

LEAVES

Make 3

With CC3 and larger hk, ch 7—foundation made.

Rnd 1: Side 1: Sc in 2nd ch from hk, hdc in next ch, dc in next 3 ch, (2 hdc, ch 2) in last ch, sc in 2nd ch from hk—picot made, 2 hdc in last ch of foundation; *9 sts, not counting picot* Rotate work, cont on opposite side of foundation ch as foll:

Side 2: Dc in next 3 ch, hdc in next ch, sc in last ch. Join with sl st in first ch of rnd. *14 sts for round, not counting picot and joining sl st*

Do not fasten off.

Work tambour crochet (see page 47) up center of leaf.

FINISHING

Weave in all ends. Sew leaves to WS of flower. Glue pin closure to back of flower; secure to hat.

"Next week shall begin operations on my hat, on which you know my principal hopes of happiness depend."

—Jane Austen, in a letter to her sister

SKILL LEVEL

MATERIALS

Nashua Handknits *DayLily* (46% cotton, 31% acrylic, 23% nylon; 87 yds/ 80 m; worsted weight #4 medium): #9434 green 5 skeins

G-6 (4 mm) hk or size needed to obtain correct gauge

½ yd (.5 m) double-sided quilted lining

4" x 11½" (10 x 29 cm) cardboard (optional)

7⅝" x 5½" (19.5 x 14 cm) Purse n-alize it! #8198095 wood purse handles

Stitcher's Kit (see page 187)

GAUGE

4 sts in matt st patt = 6" (15 cm); 7 rows in matt st patt = 4" (10 cm)

FINISHED SIZES

17" x 13" (43 x 33 cm)

STITCH GUIDE

View an online video demonstrating how to create this stitch pattern at: www.stitchscene.com/tutorials

*T*uck your favorite Austen novels into this roomy bag. Generously sized and softly shaped, you'll love how this jewel-toned purse is the perfect complement to your day. Anchor it with a pair of slim pants and sleek boots and you've instantly became a fashion-forward chit.

MAT STITCH PATTERN

Foundation ch is multiple of 6 + 2.

Row 1: Sc in 2nd ch from hk, *skip 2 ch, [(dc, ch 1) twice, dc—fan made] in next ch, skip 2 ch, sc in next ch; rep from * across, turn.

Row 2: Ch 4 (count as dc and ch 1), dc in first sc, skip 1 dc, sc in next dc, *[(dc, ch 1) twice, dc] in next sc, skip 1 dc, sc in next dc; rep from * across ending (dc, ch 1, dc) in last sc, turn.

Row 3: Ch 1 (do not count as st), sc in first dc, *[(dc, ch 1), twice, dc] in next sc, skip 1 dc, sc in next dc; rep from * across, turn.

Rep Rows 2-3 for st patt.

Note: Ch 1 at beg of row does not count as st throughout.

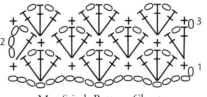

Mat Stitch Pattern Chart

stitch key
o = chain (ch)
+ = single crochet (sc)
T = double crochet (dc)

FRONT/BACK

Make 2

Ch 56.

Row 1: Sc in 2nd ch from hk, *skip 2 ch, [(dc, ch 1) twice, dc] in next ch—fan made, skip 2 ch, sc in next ch; rep from * across, turn. *9 fans*

Row 2: Ch 4 (count as dc and ch 1), dc in first sc, skip 1 dc, sc in next dc, *fan in next sc, skip 1 dc, sc in next dc; rep from * across, (dc, ch 1, dc) in last sc, turn. *8 fans*

Row 3: Ch 4, dc in first dc, sc in next ch-1 sp, *fan in next sc, skip 1 dc, sc in next dc; rep from * across ending last sc in closest ch of tch, (dc, ch 1, dc) in next ch, turn. *9 fans*

Row 4: Ch 1, sc in first dc, *fan in next sc, skip 1 dc, sc in next dc; rep from * across to last sc, fan in sc, sk 1 ch of tch, sc in next ch, turn. *10 fans*

Row 5: Rep Row 2. *9 fans*

Row 6: Rep Row 3. *10 fans*

Row 7–21: Rep Rows 4–6 for 5 times. *15 fans*

FIRST SIDE SHAPING

Row 22 (short row): Ch 1, sc in first dc, *fan in next sc, skip 1 dc, sc in next dc; rep from * 6 times more, turn leaving last st unworked. *7 fans*

Row 23: Ch 1, sc in first sc, skip 1 dc, sc in next dc, skip next dc, *fan in next sc, skip 1 dc, sc in next dc; rep from * across ending with fan in last sc, turn. *7 fans*

Row 24: Ch 1, sc in first dc, fan in next sc, skip 1 dc, sc in next dc; rep from * 5 times more, turn. *6 fans*

Row 25: Rep Row 23. *6 fans*

Fasten off.

OPPOSITE SIDE SHAPING

Join yarn to opposite edge and rep Rows 22–25.

FINISHING

Working from outer edge to center of Front, pin three evenly spaced pleats on each side—6 pleats made. Sew across top of pleats with needle and yarn. Rep with Back.

Using flat purse (pleats closed) as template, cut 2 pieces of quilted fabric for lining and sew tog. Sew Front and Back tog EXCEPT top edge. Work 1 Row sc along top edge. Place a piece of 4" x 11 ½" (10 x 29 cm) cardboard in bottom to create gusset. With hand sewing needle and thread, sew lining to purse interior. Cut 2 rectangles from lining, fold and seam each one with WS tog. Turn RS out, hem raw edges and use these 2 rectangles to sew purse handles to lining.

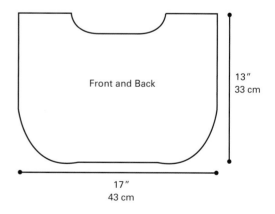

Front and Back

13"
33 cm

17"
43 cm

CHAPTER 2

The Comfort of Home: Home Accessories

"There is nothing like staying
at home for real comfort."

—*Emma*

"Well surely Miss Austen, you cannot mean for Catherine to travel alone. And by stage at that! Snip out those shocking words or I shall leave the room this instant!"

"If only you would Marianne," Miss Austen answered, wishing to focus on Catherine's story. She rested her head upon her desk. After a moment she asked me to pour her some tea.

"But there must be a more suitable way for you to write about Catherine's eviction from Northanger Abbey." Marianne entreated. "Her parents might suddenly arrive, or perhaps Mr. and Mrs. Allen will be traveling past and decide to look in on Catherine." She circled the sitting room, her great spirit of discomposure preventing her from sitting.

"Perchance" said Fanny, who was busily arranging her aunt's work and never one to agree with any breach of propriety. "Mr. Tilney shall arrive home from his business just in time to learn of what is happening?"

"Yes!" exclaimed Marianne, snapping her fingers. "And he shall tell the General that Catherine will never be leaving Northanger Abbey for she is to be his wife!"

I handed Miss Austen her tea which she thanked me for kindly and then enjoyed, seemingly oblivious to the rising hysterics around her.

Softly clearing her throat, Emma spoke: "While I do not share the same exuberance as Marianne, Miss Austen—nor do I suppose to tell you how you should write your stories—I do concur with Marianne and Fanny on the matter of this simply not being acceptable etiquette for a man like General Tilney—to force Catherine to travel by public coach without a chaperone is quite shocking and completely unexpected, I daresay." She paused, frowning at the tasseled pillow she was seaming. "One would expect quite better from a man of his station."

All the while, Miss Austen continued to sip her tea.

"I shall be quite all right," Catherine said, the timidity in her voice betraying the confidence of her words. "It is an adventure really," she added. But her mind, rich with the imaginative terrors that quickly made their home there, forced her to pause before continuing. "There are worse things to endure than riding in a public coach. I am sure of it. I believe there can be no doubt of my arriving home safely."

"How shall you bear it Catherine?" Marianne sighed, sinking heavily into the settee. "I could not. Not ever."

"Perhaps," I offered, "Catherine will not suffer anything too untoward as long as she has a carriage blanket wrapped about her." We quickly set to work on one.

SKILL LEVEL

MATERIALS

Patons *Decor* (75% acrylic, 25% wool; 208 yds/190 m; worsted weight #4 medium): #87714 barn red (MC) 7 skeins; #87631 taupe (CC1) 3 skeins; #87614 winter white (CC2) 3 skeins

H-8 (5 mm) hk or size needed to obtain correct gauge

Stitcher's Kit (see page 187)

GAUGE

7 ch-sp (dc and ch 1) and 6 rows in double crochet mesh st patt = 4" (10 cm) unblocked, not woven

FINISHED SIZES

58" x 65" (142 x 162.5 cm) excluding 3" (7.5 cm) long fringe at each end.

Note: Loose or tight weaving affects finished size.

STITCH GUIDE

View an online video demonstrating how to create this stitch pattern at: www.stitchscene.com/tutorials

*T*hough this beautiful blanket looks complicated, it is actually very easy. Worked in a double crochet mesh stitch, this afghan works up quickly and is finished by vertically weaving yarn through the mesh stitches to create a delightful plaid pattern with sumptuous drape worthy of any afternoon picnic or nap.

DOUBLE CROCHET MESH STITCH PATTERN

Foundation ch is multiple of 2 + 4.

Row 1: Dc in 6th ch from hk, *ch 1, skip 1 ch, dc in next ch; rep from * across, turn.

Row 2: Ch 4, skip first dc, dc in next dc, *ch 1, dc in next dc; rep from * across ending ch 1, skip 1 ch of tch, dc in next ch of tch, turn.

Rep Row 2 for st patt.

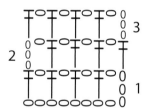

stitch key
o = chain (ch)
Ŧ = double crochet (dc)

Double Crochet Mesh Stitch Pattern Chart

MESH BASE

With MC, ch 220.

Row 1: Dc in 6th ch from hk (count as ch-sp), *ch 1, skip 1 ch, dc in next ch; rep from * across, turn. *108 ch-sp*

Row 2: Ch 4, skip first dc, dc in next dc, *ch 1, dc in next dc; rep from * across ending ch 1, skip 1 ch of turning ch, dc in next ch.

Note: Fasten off first yarn when changing col in last st of row and leave tails for weaving in.

Cont work even (rep Row 2) AT SAME TIME change col as foll:

Rows 3–11: Odd rows in CC2, even rows in CC1.

Rows 12–20: MC.

Rows 21–92: Rep from ** for 4 times.

Rows 93–103: Rep from ** to end of Row 13.

Fasten off.

WEAVING

Thread tapestry needle with 2 strands MC, each 80" (2.1 m) long. With foundation ch oriented horizontally and closest, beg in first row of lower right-hand corner by weaving up in first hole in mesh, down in hole immediately above. Cont weaving in and out of mesh to end of Row 103. Cut yarn leaving at least 6" (15 cm) tail at top and bottom edges (for fringe). Pull taut after working each column. Weave 2 strands MC through next column to left of column just made, weaving down in first hole, up in next hole, and so on. Cont weaving as established changing col as foll:

*Next 3 columns CC1, 2 columns MC, 3 columns CC1,** 8 columns MC; rep from * across to opposite edge of blanket, ending last rep at ** and ending 2 columns MC.

FRINGE

With afghan oriented as before and beg at lower-right edge, cut 2 strands of yarn, each 10" (25.5 cm) long, in same col as yarn woven through mesh at that point. Fold strands over bottom foundation ch, knot tog (include weaving yarn tails). Rep in each hole in mesh across bottom and top of afghan. Trim fringe to 3" (7.5 cm) long.

❧ MARIANNE'S MEMENTO BOARD ❧

*A*re you the sentimental type or know someone who is? This memento board makes the perfect gift for yourself or another. Honor your favorite memories by displaying in a prominent place those treasures that bring a smile to your face. This memento board serves as an eclectic way to display your favorite jewelry, photos, and notes while also showcasing your crochet talents; doing double duty as a fantastic décor piece—your own cherished piece of artwork—it lends a certain heirloom chic to any room.

CORONET STITCH PATTERN

See chart page 61.

Foundation ch is multiple of 7 + 4.

Row 1: Skip 3 ch (count as dc), dc in next ch, (ch 3, sl st in top of dc just made)—picot made, 2 dc in same ch, *skip 6 ch, (3 dc, picot, ch 1, dc, picot, 2 dc) in next ch—coronet made; rep from * to last 7 ch, skip 6 ch, (3 dc, picot, dc) in last ch, turn.

Row 2: Ch 3 (count as dc), dc in first st, *ch 3, (dc, picot, dc) in ch-1 sp at center of next coronet—picot V st made; rep from * ending ch 3, 2 dc in top of tch, turn.

Row 3: Ch 2 (count as hdc), skip first 2 sts, *coronet in next ch-3 sp, skip next picot V st; rep from * ending coronet in last ch-3 sp, hdc in top of tch, turn.

Row 4: Ch 4 (count as dc and ch 1), *picot V st in ch-sp at center of next coronet, ch 3; rep from * ending picot V st in last coronet, ch 1, dc in top of tch, turn.

Row 5: Ch 3 (count as dc), skip first st, (dc, picot, 2 dc) in first ch-sp, *skip next picot V st, coronet in next ch-3 sp; rep from * ending skip last picot V st, 3 dc in next ch, picot, dc in next ch of tch, turn.

Rep Rows 2-5 for st patt.

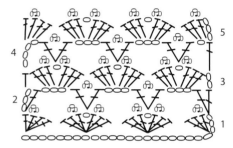

Coronet Stitch Pattern Chart

stitch key
◦ = chain (ch)
⊤ = half double crochet (hdc)
Ŧ = double crochet (dc)
🎀 = picot

MEMENTO BOARD

Note: End-of-row st counts do not include partial coronets at beg and end of rows.

With MC, ch 144.

Row 1: Skip 3 ch (count as dc), dc in next ch, (ch 3, sl st in top of dc just made)—picot made, 2 dc in same ch, *skip 6 ch, (3 dc, picot, ch 1, dc, picot, 2 dc in next ch—coronet made; rep from * to last 7 ch, skip 6 ch, (3 dc, picot, dc) in last ch, turn. *19 coronets*

Row 2: With CC1, ch 3 (count as dc), dc in first st, ch 3, (dc, picot, dc) in ch-1 sp at center of next coronet—picot V st made; rep from * ending ch 3, 2 dc in top of tch, turn.

Row 3: With MC, ch 2 (count as hdc), skip first 2 sts, *coronet

in next ch-3 sp, skip next picot V st; rep from * ending coronet in last ch-3 sp, hdc in tch, turn.

Row 4: With CC1, ch 4 (count as dc and ch 1), *picot V st in ch-sp at center of next coronet, ch 3; rep from * ending picot V st in last coronet, ch 1, dc in top of tch, turn.

Row 5: With MC, ch 3 (count as dc), skip first st, (dc, picot, 2 dc) in first ch-sp, *skip next picot V st, coronet in next ch-3 sp; rep from * ending skip last picot V st, 3 dc in next ch, picot, dc in next ch of tch, turn.

Next 43 Rows: Rep Rows 2–5. Fasten off.

FINISHING

Weave in ends. Steam block to 20" x 24" (51 x 61 cm). Using frame closure as guide, cut foamcore to same size minus ¼" (6 mm) on each side. Using spray adhesive, lightly glue quilt batting to top of foamcore. Trim even with edges of foamcore. Place satin fabric over batting, wrap over edges of foamcore and secure tightly on underside. Place crochet piece over satin, wrap over edges of foamcore and secure with spray adhesive on WS. Place work in frame holding all in place with original frame backing.

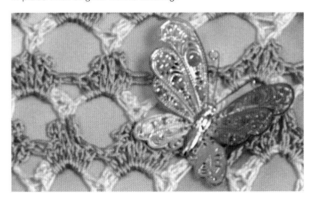

Sense or Sensibility—which sister are you?

1. The 3" (7.5 cm) heels in your closet seal the style deal on the outfit you are wearing, but your "like walking on marshmallows" skimmers would work almost as well. Which do you choose?

    a. The heels, style over comfort every day.

    b. The skimmers of course.

    c. 3" (7.5 cm) heels? They aren't even in my closet.

2. Do you change your Facebook status to single within fifteen minutes of breaking up with your boyfriend?

3. What is your age limit when searching for an eligible bachelor?

    a. Same age to five years older

    b. Up to ten years older

    c. A man is a man—no expiration date

4. If you don't hear from your beau for more than a week, do you start planning the relationship's funeral?

5. Have you ever spoken the words "I love you" aloud to a man before he said the words to you?

6. You meet the man of your dreams online. You . . .

    a. Set up a date within the next week—there is no time to waste.

    b. Repeat to yourself: "Good things happen to those who wait."

7. Have you ever cleaned the shower, even just a little bit, while taking one?

Check your results on page 203.

SKILL LEVEL

MATERIALS

Kertzer *Northern Worsted* (100% acrylic; 230 yds/210 m; worsted weight #4 medium): #0904 winter white (MC) 3 skeins; #0101 goldensand (CC1) 2 skeins; #0286 harbor haze (CC2) 3 skeins

G-6 (4 mm) hk or size needed to obtain correct gauge

Quilt batting

Polyester fiberfill for bolster only

Square pillow form or additional polyester fiberfill

Tassel maker

Stitcher's Kit (see page 187)

GAUGE

12 sc and 13 rows = 4" (10 cm)

FINISHED SIZES

Square is 16" (40.5 cm). Bolster has width of 15" and circumference of 16" (38 x 40.5 cm)

STITCH GUIDE

View an online video demonstrating how to create this stitch pattern at: www.stitch scene.com/tutorials

*Y*our love affair with Austen novels continues as you recreate the look of a Regency sitting room with help from these tasseled pillows. The lace overlay on the square pillow calls to mind the delicate lattice work upon which English Ivy grows; the bolster features ruffled lace accents—a popular trimming of the time, just as at home today. Both pillows bring added texture and dimension to your living quarters, providing a sophisticated finish to your home.

PICOT TRELLIS STITCH PATTERN

Foundation is multiple of 5 + 2.

Row 1: Sc in 2nd ch from hk, *ch 5, skip 4 ch, sc in next ch; rep from * across, turn.

Row 2: Ch 5, [sc, ch 3, sc] in 3rd ch of first ch-5 arch—picot made, *ch 5, picot in 3rd ch of next ch-5 arch; rep from * across ending ch 2, dc in last sc, turn.

Row 3: Ch 1 (do not count as st), sc in first st, *ch 5, skip picot, picot in 3rd ch of next ch-5 arch; rep from * across ending ch 5, skip picot, sc in tch arch, turn. Rep Rows 2–3 for st patt.

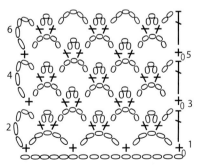

Picot Trellis Stitch Pattern Chart

stitch key
o = chain (ch)
+ = single crochet (sc)
$\mathcal{T}$ = double crochet (dc)

SPLIT SINGLE CROCHET STITCH (ssc)

Work as for basic sc EXCEPT insert hk through work between 2 vertical strands of sc in previous row.

Note: Ch 1 at beg of row does not count as st throughout.

COVER

Make 2

With MC, ch 49.

Row 1: Sc in 2nd ch from hk and each ch across, turn. *48 sc*

Rows 2–52: Ch 1, sc in each st across, turn.

Fasten off.

LATTICE OVERLAY

Make 2

With CC2, ch 42.

Row 1: Sc in 2nd ch from hk, *ch 5, skip 4 ch, sc in next ch; rep from * across, turn. *8 ch-5 arches*

Row 2: Ch 5, [sc, ch 3, sc] in 3rd ch of first ch-5 arch—picot made, *ch 5, picot in 3rd ch of next ch-5 arch; rep from * across ending ch 2, dc in last sc, turn.

Row 3: Ch 1, sc in first st, *ch 5, skip picot, picot in 3rd ch of next ch-5 arch; rep from * across ending ch 5, skip picot, sc in tch arch, turn.

Next 20 Rows: Rep Rows 2–3.

Fasten off.

FINISHING

Weave in ends. Steam block cover and overlay pieces to 16¼" (41 cm) square. Seam cover pieces tog on 3 sides. Cut quilt batting to 16" x 32" (40.5 x 81.5 cm). Fold in half and insert inside seamed cover to ensure smooth finish. Stuff fiberfill or pillow form inside batting. Whipstitch closed open side of cover. Place overlay on each side of pillow. Whipstitch edges tog. With CC1, make four tassels, each 3" (7.5 cm) long, wrapping yarn around tassel maker 11 times. Sew one to corner of each pillow.

BOLSTER

Notes: Unless noted, there is no ch 1 or tch between rnds. Pm in first st to note beg of rnd being sure to move marker up with each new rnd.

With CC2, ch 2.

Rnd 1: 6 sc in 2nd ch from hk.

Rnd 2: 2 ssc in each sc around. *12 sts*

Rnd 3: *Ssc in next 2 sc, 2 ssc in next sc—inc made; rep from * around. *18 sts*

Rnd 4: *Ssc in next 3 sc, 2 ssc in next sc; rep from * around. *24 sts*

Rnd 5: *Ssc in next 4 sc, 2 ssc in next sc; rep from * around. *30 sts*

Rnd 6: *Ssc in next 5 sc, 2 ssc in next sc; rep from * around. *36 sts*

Rnd 7: *Ssc in next 6 sc, 2 ssc in next sc; rep from * around. *42 sts*

Rnd 8: *Ssc in next 7 sc, 2 ssc in next sc; rep from * around. *48 sts*

End CC2.

Rnd 9: With MC, ch 1 (do not count as st), working in blo, sc around, join with sl st in first ch.

Rnds 10–17: Ch 1 (do not count as st), ssc around, join with sl st in first ch.

End MC.

Rnds 18–26: With CC2 rep Rows 9–17.

Next 27 Rnds: Rep Rnds 9–26 alternating colors as established. Remove marker.

Fasten off.

OPPOSITE END

With CC2, ch 2.

Rep Rnds 1–8.

Fasten off.

BOLSTER ASSEMBLY

Weave in ends. Line bolster with quilt batting and stuff with polyester fiberfill as for Square Pillow. With pillow end facing, whipstitch (see page 199) Rnd 8 of Opposite End to flo of Rnd 53.

FIRST RUFFLE

Note: Pm in tch to note beg of rnd being sure to move marker up with each new rnd. Ch 1 at beg of rnd does not count as st. Attach CC1 to flo of Bolster Rnd 9.

Rnd 1: Ch 1, sc flo in each st around, join with sl st in first sc, turn. *48 sts*

Rnd 2: Ch 1, sc in first sc, *ch 1, sc in next st; rep from * across, join with sl st in first sc, turn. *48 ch-sp*

Rnd 3: Ch 3, sc in first sc, *ch 3, sc in next st; rep from * across, join with sl st in first sc, turn.

Rnd 4: Ch 5, sc in first sc, *ch 5, sc in next st; rep from * across, join with sl st in first sc. Remove marker.

Fasten off.

SECOND RUFFLE

Attach yarn to (unworked) flo of st in Rnd 18 and work as for First Ruffle.

NEXT 4 RUFFLES

Add ruffle to each color change of Bolster body and work as for First Ruffle.

FINISHING

With CC1, make 2 tassels, each 3" (7.5 cm) long, by wrapping tassel maker 11 times and secure to center of ends. Weave in ends.

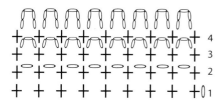

Web Ruffle Stitch Pattern Chart

stitch key
○ = chain (ch)
+ = single crochet (sc)

SKILL LEVEL

MATERIALS

Rowan *Silky Tweed* (80% lambswool, 20% silk; 137 yds/125 m; aran weight #3 light): 12 skeins each of #752 ember (MC); #759 mardigras (CC1)

G-6 (4 mm) hk or size needed to obtain correct gauge

Tassel maker

Stitcher's Kit (see page 187)

GAUGE

7 ch-sp (dc and ch 1) and 6 rows in double crochet mesh st patt = 4" (10 cm) unblocked, not woven

FINISHED SIZES

53" x 63" (135 x 160 cm) excluding 5" (13 cm) tassels at each end

Note: Finished size may vary depending on how tightly woven strands are drawn through mesh.

STITCH GUIDE

View an online video demonstrating how to create this stitch pattern at: www.stitchscene.com/tutorials

ave you been searching high and low for a crocheted project that the man in your life will truly be happy to receive? Search no more. This woven afghan, worked in rustic silky tweed, is sure to please even the most discerning of Mr. Knightleys in your life. Stitched in a simple double crochet grid woven with long lengths of yarn, then finished with tasseled edges, it creates a masculine texture he will definitely take pleasure in. Use his favorite team's colors to increase his enjoyment. Go ahead and splurge—on him or yourself. The beautiful results are worth it.

DOUBLE CROCHET MESH STITCH PATTERN

Foundation chain is multiple of 2 + 4.

Row 1: Dc in 6th ch from hk, *ch 1, skip 1 ch, dc in next ch; rep from * across, turn.

Row 2: Ch 4, skip first dc, dc in next dc, *ch 1, dc in next dc; rep from * across ending ch 1, skip 1 ch of tch, dc in next ch of tch, turn.

Rep Row 2 for st patt.

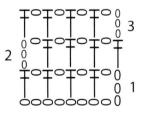

Double Crochet Mesh Stitch Pattern Chart

stitch key
○ = chain (ch)
+ = single crochet (sc)

MESH BASE

With MC, ch 200.

Row 1: Dc in 6th ch from hk (count as ch-sp), *ch 1, skip 1 ch, dc in next ch; rep from * across, turn. *98 ch-sps*

Row 2: Ch 4, skip first dc, dc in next dc, *ch 1, dc in next dc; rep from * across ending ch 1, skip 1 ch of tch, dc in next ch of tch AT SAME TIME change col to CC1 (see page 196), turn. Fasten off MC leaving 6" (15 cm) tails. With CC1 cont as foll:

Rows 3: Ch 4, skip first dc, dc in next dc, *ch 1, dc in next dc;

rep from * across ending ch 1, skip 1 ch of tch, dc in next ch of tch, turn.

Row 4: Ch 4, skip first dc, dc in next dc, *ch 1, dc in next dc; rep from * across ending ch 1, skip 1 ch of tch, dc in next ch of tch AT SAME TIME change col to MC.

Rows 5–102: Rep Rows 3–4. Fasten off.

Weave in ends EXCEPT along foundation ch and Row 102.

WEAVING

Thread tapestry needle with 3 strands MC, each 90" (2.3 m) long. With foundation ch horizontal and closest, beg in first row of lower right-hand corner by weaving up in first hole in mesh, down in hole immediately above. Cont weaving in and out of mesh to Row 102. Cut yarn leaving at least 6" (15 cm) tail at top and bottom edges (for fringe). Pull taut after working each column. Weave 3 strands MC through next column to left of column just made, weaving down in first hole, up in next hole, and so on. Cont weaving as established changing col every 2 columns (*2 columns CC1, 2 columns MC; rep from * across).

TASSELS

Make 68 tassels (34 for each edge), each 5" (13 cm) long by wrapping yarn 18 times around tassel maker.

FINISHING

With afghan oriented as before, tie tassel to first ch-sp of foundation ch and hide tassel ties and weaving tails by threading tails into tassel. Cont attaching tassel in every 2nd ch-sp along foundation ch and Row 102. Weave in loose ends.

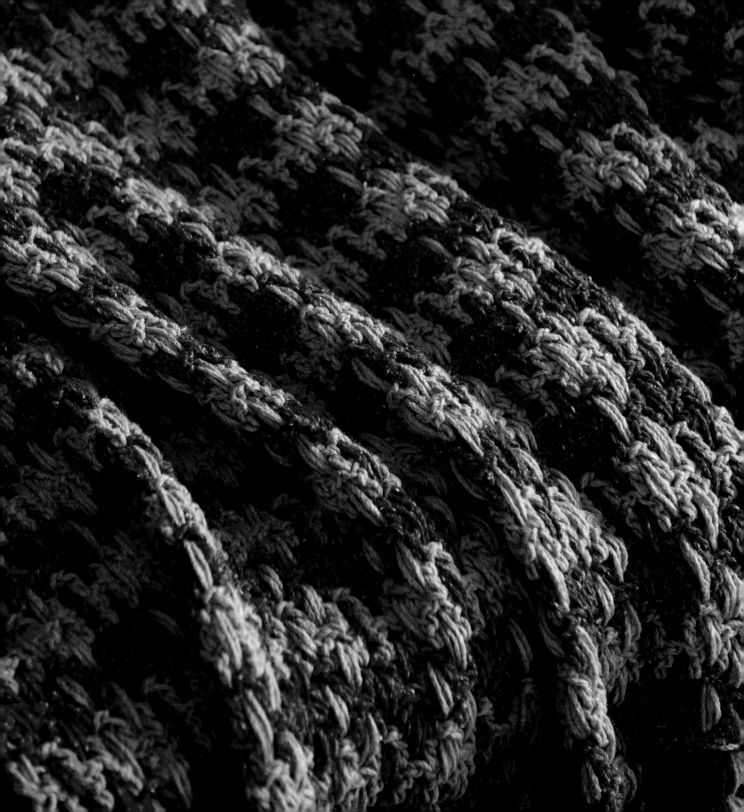

SKILL LEVEL

MATERIALS

Brown Sheep *Burley Spun* (100% wool; 130 yds / 121 m; roving weight #6 super bulky): 2 skeins each of #BS215 tormented teal (MC); #BS08 wild oak (CC1)

Q (15.75 mm) hk or size needed to obtain correct gauge

Stitcher's Kit (see page 187)

GAUGE

6 sts and 7 rows in ssc = 4" (10 cm)

FINISHED SIZES

23½" x 32½" (60 x 82.5 cm)

STITCH GUIDE

View an online video demonstrating how to create this stitch pattern at: www.stitchscene.com/tutorials

*H*ousehold chores become less wearisome with this cushy addition underfoot. The thick, chunky ply of this yarn is reminiscent of roving—one can almost see flocks of sheep grazing on the hillsides next to Barton Cottage while the yarn slides through your fingers. Akin to the knit stockinette, this crochet stitch is easy to work once learned, and it showcases the versatility of crochet. Practical, yet plush, this rug is equally Elinor and Marianne.

SPLIT SINGLE CROCHET STITCH (ssc)

Work as for basic sc EXCEPT insert hk between 2 vertical strands of sc in previous row.

Notes: Fasten off at each color change. Leave at least 4" (10 cm) tail (for fringe) when fastening off and joining colors throughout.

Do not to skip first st of each row; 2 vertical strands can be difficult to see.

RUG

With MC, ch 50.

Row 1: Sc in 2nd ch from hk and in each ch across. *49 sts*

Row 2: Ch 1, ssc (see page 70) across.

Fasten off.

Cont work even in ssc (rep Row 2) to 23½" (60 cm) from beg
AT SAME TIME change col as foll: 3 rows CC1, 1 row MC, 2
rows CC1, 2 rows MC, 1 row CC1, 2 rows MC, 4 rows CC1,
1 row MC, 3 rows CC1, 2 rows MC, 1 row CC1, 2 rows MC,
4 rows CC1, 3 rows MC, 1 row CC1, 1 row MC, 1 row CC1,
1 row MC, 3 rows CC1, 1 row MC.

Fasten off.

FINISHING

Weave in ends EXCEPT along short edges. Cut 8" (2 cm)
lengths of yarn and knot to make fringe along short edges,
trapping ends in the knotting.

SKILL LEVEL

MATERIALS

Cascade *Ultra Pima* (100% pima cotton; 220 yds/202 m; dk weight #3 light): #3718 natural 1 skein

G-6 (4 mm) hk or size needed to obtain correct gauge

E-4 (3.5 mm) hk

DMC Linen Floss in L159 sky blue, L435 copper, L437 peach, L833 flax, L3012 sage green

Stitcher's Kit (see page 187)

GAUGE

8 cluster sts and 7 rows = 4" (10 cm) with larger hk

FINISHED SIZES

9¼" x 5" (23.5 x 13 cm) with flap closed.

STITCH GUIDE

View an online video demonstrating how to create this stitch pattern at: www.stitchscene.com/tutorials

*D*uring Regency times, ladies kept their important letters, notes of sale, and such in a tri-fold pocket book similar to this one. You will find it a special place to store treasured mementos from your Mr. Darcy or Captain Wentworth. Rustically embroidered in tambour crochet for a period look, it's the perfect pocket for those special items you wish to honor by keeping them in a fine place.

DOUBLE CROCHET CLUSTER STITCH

Yo, insert hk in st, yo and draw through st, yo and draw through 2 lps on hk, *yo, insert hk in same st, yo and draw through st, yo and draw through 2 lps on hk; rep from * once more, yo and draw through all 4 lps on hk.

REVERSE SINGLE CROCHET STITCH (rev sc)

Working from left to right, *insert hk in st to right, work sc (yo and draw through st, yo and draw through 2 lps on hk).

TAMBOUR CROCHET STITCHING

Start chain on crocheted fabric surface with yarn beneath finished work at beg of desired design line. Insert hk through fabric, yo and draw through lp. *Working along design line, insert hk through crocheted fabric slightly forward from last position, yo and draw lp through fabric and through lp on hk–surface ch made. Rep from * along design line. At end of line cut working yarn, remove hk from last lp, place hk underneath fabric and draw through lp. Draw yarn tail through lp to fasten off on WS.

ENVELOPE

With larger hk, ch 39.

Row 1: Cluster (see page 72) in 5th ch from hk, *skip 1 ch, cluster in next ch; rep from * across, turn. *18 clusters*

Row 2: Ch 3, cluster in each cluster across, turn.

Next 17 Rows: Rep Row 2.

FLAP

Row 20: Ch 1, sc in first two clusters, cluster in each cluster across to last 2, sc in each of last 2 clusters, turn. *14 clusters*

Row 21: Sl st in first 2 sc, sc in next two clusters, cluster in each cluster across to last 2 sc, sc in each of last 2 clusters, turn. *10 clusters*

Next 2 Rows: Rep Row 21. *2 clusters*

Fasten off.

FINISHING

Fold work across width between Rows 8 and 9 with WS tog. Beg at bottom left, rev sc (see page 72) along left edge of envelope inserting larger hk through both layers for each st. Fasten off. With front of envelope facing, beg at top right fold line, rev sc along right edge of envelope inserting hk through both layers for each st. Fasten off. With RS of flap facing, rev sc through single layer around flap edge. Fasten off.

With smaller hk, tambour crochet (see page 72) design at right working with all 6 strands of embroidery floss. Weave in ends. Steam block to finished measurements.

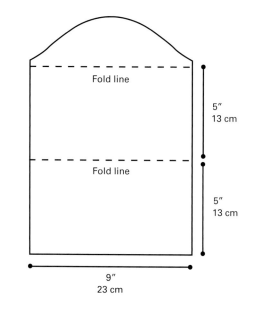

Fold line

Fold line

5"
13 cm

5"
13 cm

9"
23 cm

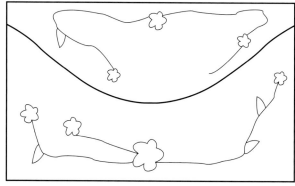

Tambour Crochet Diagram

Letters

Jane Austen often used letters to convey plot turns in her novels. See how Austentatious you are—how many are you able to connect the correct writer with the recipient?

1. "Be not alarmed, Madam, on receiving this letter, by the apprehension of its containing any repetition of those sentiments, or renewal of those offers, which were last night so disgusting to you . . . "
   a. Mr. Collins to Elizabeth
   b. Captain Wentworth to Anne
   c. Mr. Darcy to Elizabeth
   c. Mr. Tilney to Catherine

2. "I can listen no longer in silence. I must speak to you by such means as are within my reach. You pierce my soul. I am half agony, half hope. Tell me not that I am too late, that such precious feelings are gone forever."
   a. Mr. Darcy to Elizabeth
   b. Mr. Willoughby to Marianne
   c. Edmund Bertram to Fanny
   d. Captain Wentworth to Anne

3. "Dear Sir, Being very sure I have long lost your affections, I have thought myself at liberty to bestow my own on another, and have no doubt of being as happy with him as I once used to think I might be with you; but I scorn to accept a hand while the heart was another's."
   a. Mary Crawford to Edmund
   b. Lucy Steele to Edward
   c. Marianne to Willoughby
   d. Fanny to Henry

4. "My Dear Madam, I have just had the honour of receiving your letter, for which I beg to return my sincere acknowledgments. I am much concerned to find there was anything in my behavior last night that did not meet your approbation; and though I am quite at a loss to discover in what point I could be so unfortunate as to offend you, I entreat your forgiveness of what I can assure you to have been perfectly unintentional."
   a. Mr. Bingley to Jane
   b. Mr. Darcy to Elizabeth
   c. Mr. Willoughby to Marianne
   d. Mr. Edward Ferrar to Elinor

Check your results on page 203.

Crossed in Love: Head-to-toe Patterns to Captivate your Heart

"Next to being married, a girl likes to be crossed in love a little now and then."

—Mr. Bennet, *Pride and Prejudice*

E verything was not going as it should. Chaos reigned in the small sitting room, yet all except me appeared oblivious. The mastermind of the hubbub appeared on my right. "It is all going very well, is it not?" she asked, the poised elegance of this young woman portraying not the slightest hint of her willfulness.

"Emma," I began. "I do not think this is what Miss Austen had in mind when she said business as usual until she returned."

"Yes. Well I possess a keen power of perception and I was quite aware of what Miss Austen was hinting at." Emma lowered her voice to a murmur, "I would never share this with just anyone," she began, "but she has been having quite her share of troubles in the match-making department—her own included. It is only right that she would come to me for a bit of assistance and naturally I understand her wish to remain quite discreet about it."

"Quite honestly" she continued, "it was no easy feat for even me to achieve this." With a sweep of her hand, she said, "Without Mr. Darcy's assistance, I do not believe I would have succeeded in separating Mr. Bingley and Miss Bennet. They are entirely too much alike in their exceeding kindness. Their household would be quite poorly managed, as Jane noted but did nothing about. And I believe I have done them both no small favor in pairing them up with Fanny and Mr. Ferrar. Fanny's practicality will nicely balance Mr. Bingley's kindness and Miss Bennet's amiable nature would better serve Edward Ferrar's position in the clergy. And there is the added benefit that she is used to living with less."

"So is Elinor and she is just as kind," I pointed out. Where was Miss Austen? I thought, wishing I could wave my hook around and simply make things right. "I really don't think you should be alter-"

"Fear not. I am quite certain this is what Miss Austen wishes. Did she herself not give me the aptitude for match making? I am much more at ease now with these connections. I never did feel that Mr. Frank Churchill and Miss Jane Fairfax was quite the match. I believe he would be much better served with the youthful vivacity of Catherine. And look," she said, "Darcy is fascinated by Anne. I believe their restrained temperaments to be quite better suited for one another."

I gazed in the direction she noted. Mr. Darcy looked as uninterested as ever, and Anne, dear Anne appeared as if she had just lost her entire fortune at one hand of whist. She stared at Captain Wentworth, who had

a captivated audience in Marianne, whose curiosity about high-sea adventures had no restraint.

"My next challenge is to help Miss Austen acquire a husband of her own. She really has remained clueless."

"I don't think there will be any need for you to trouble yourself with husband hunting on my account, Emma," said Miss Austen, approaching from behind. Taking several moments to survey the room, Miss Austen winced when she saw Elinor, too polite to interrupt Mr. Collins's lengthy eulogy of his humble parsonage, glancing about the room for any excuse to quit his company.

"It would be no trouble to find you a suitor, Miss Austen. Well actually, there might be some degree of difficulty with your" Emma paused for a moment, deciding it best not to proceed with that line of thought. "It would be my great pleasure, actually," she finished.

"Well," said Miss Austen, smoothing the lines of her dress, "I see you took the liberty of matching up Elizabeth Bennet with Mr. Knightley. I had not thought of that pair, but now that you have put the two together before my eyes I can see how well suited they are for one another. Well done Emma!"

Emma turned to the couple at attention. She watched as Elizabeth held the scarf she had been stitching up to Mr. Knightley's chiseled features. A confounded expression befell Emma before she took several hurried steps toward them.

SKILL LEVEL

MATERIALS

J&P Coats *Royale Fashion Crochet Thread Size 3* (100% mercerised cotton; 150 yds/137 m): #871 plum (MC) 8 (9, 10, 11, 12) balls; #226 natural (CC1) 2 (2, 2, 3, 3) balls

D-3 (3.25 mm) hk or size needed to obtain correct gauge

Stitcher's Kit (see page 187)

GAUGE

20 hdc and 12 rows = 4" (10 cm)

FINISHED SIZES

XS (S, M, L, 1X) has bust circumference of 33½ (36½, 39½, 42½, 46)"/ 85 (93, 100.5, 108, 117) cm

STITCH GUIDE

View an online video demonstrating how to create this stitch pattern at: www.stitchscene.com/tutorials

*R*egency glam marries modern design in this gorgeous blouse with a fit that gently kisses the body. Lace cuffs add a touch of romance, as does the embellished inset comprised of roses, violets, and leaf sprays. This top would look just as at home paired with jeans and sleek boots as it does with this striking ruffled skirt.

FRONT POST SINGLE CROCHET STITCH (fpsc)

Insert hk around post of specified stitch (from front to back and then back to front) of row below, work as for single crochet.

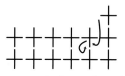

Front post single crochet stitch

HALF DOUBLE CROCHET DECREASE STITCH (hdc2tog)

[Yo hk, insert hk in next st, yo and draw through lp] twice, yo and draw through all 5 lps on hk.

MID-ROW COLOR CHANGE

To change col, work to last last yo of last st of MC; yo with CC1 and draw through all lps on hk to complete st. Twist CC1 over MC. DO NOT carry MC across back of work. Use separate ball of yarn for each col block. Twist MC and CC1 at each color change to prevent hole in work.

TAMBOUR CROCHET STITCHING

Start chain on crocheted fabric surface with yarn beneath finished work at beg of desired design line. Insert hk through fabric, yo and draw through lp. *Working along design line, insert hk through crocheted fabric slightly forward from last

position, yo and draw lp through fabric and through lp on hk–surface ch made. Rep from * along design line. At end of line cut working yarn, remove hk from last lp, place hk underneath fabric and draw through lp. Draw yarn tail through lp to fasten off on WS.

Note: Ch 1 and/or sl st(s) at beg of rows do not count as st(s) throughout.

BACK

With MC, ch 88 (96, 104, 112, 122).

Row 1: Hdc in 2nd ch from hk (count as hdc) and each ch across, turn. *87 (95, 103, 111, 121) sts*

Rows 2–5: Ch 1, hdc across, turn.

Row 6: Ch 1, hdc2tog (see page 79), hdc across to last two sts, hdc2tog, turn. *85 (93, 101, 109, 119) sts*

Row 7: Ch 1, hdc across, turn.

Next 6 (6, 6, 4, 6) Rows: Rep Rows 6 and 7 for 3 (3, 3, 2, 3) times. *79 (87, 95, 105, 113) sts*

L Only

Rows 12–13: Ch 1, hdc across, turn.

All Sizes

Next 2 (3, 1, 1, 1) Rows: Rep Row 6. *75 (81, 93, 103, 111) sts*

Next 2 (1, 1, 1, 1) Rows: Ch 1, hdc across, turn.

Next 4 (4, 8, 8, 8) Rows: Rep Rows 6 and 7 for 2 (2, 4, 4, 4) times. *71 (77, 85, 95, 103) sts*

Note: Row 21 (21, 23, 23, 23) now complete.

Next 1 (1, 1, 2, 2) Rows: Ch 1, hdc across, turn.

XS, S, M Only

Next Row: Ch 1, 2 hdc in first st, hdc across to last st, 2 hdc in last st, turn. *73 (79, 87) sts*

XS, S Only

Next 2 Rows: Rep last 2 rows. *(75, 81) sts*

All Sizes

Next 2 Rows: Ch 1, hdc across, turn.

Row 28: Ch 1, 2 hdc in first st, hdc across ending 2 hdc in last st, turn. *77 (83, 89, 97, 105) sts*

Rows 29–33: Work even with inc (rep Row 28) every 3rd row once; then every 2nd row once. *81 (87, 93, 101, 109) sts*

Next 9 (9, 9, 9, 11) Rows: Work even with inc (rep Row 28) every 3rd row for 3 times; then every 2nd row 0 (0, 0, 0, 1) time. *87 (93, 99, 107, 117) sts*

M, L Only

Next 1 Row: Rep Row 28. *(101, 109) sts*

S, M, L, 1X Only

Next (2, 4, 4, 4) Rows: Ch 1, hdc across, turn.

All Sizes

Cont with Armhole Shaping.

ARMHOLE SHAPING

Next Row: Sl st in first 4 sts, hdc across leaving last 4 sts unworked, turn. *79 (85, 93, 101, 109) sts.*

Next Row: Sl st in first 2 (2, 2, 3, 3), hdc across leaving last 2 (2, 2, 3, 3) sts unworked, turn. *75 (81, 89, 95, 103) sts*

Next Row: Sl st in first 0 (0, 1, 2, 3) st, hdc across leaving last 0 (0, 1, 2, 3) st unworked, turn. *75 (81, 87, 91, 97) sts*

Next Row: Sl st in first 1, (1, 1, 1, 2) st, hdc across leaving last 1 (1, 1, 1, 2) st unworked, turn. *73 (79, 85, 89, 93) sts*

Next Row: Sl st in first st, hdc across leaving last st unworked, turn. *71 (77, 83, 87, 91) sts*

Next Row: Sl st in first 0 (0, 0, 0, 1) st, hdc across leaving last 0 (0, 0, 0, 1) st unworked, turn. *71 (77, 83, 87, 89) sts*

Next 2 Rows: Rep last 2 rows. *69 (75, 81, 85, 85) sts*

Next Row: Sl st in first st, hdc across leaving last st unworked, turn. *67 (73, 79, 83, 83) sts*

Next 2 Rows: Ch 1, hdc in each st across, turn.

Next Row: Sl st in first 0 (1, 1, 1, 1) st, hdc across leaving last 0 (1, 1, 1, 1) st unworked, turn. *67 (71, 77, 81, 81) sts*

Next 8 (10, 13, 14, 14) Rows: Ch 1, hdc in each st across, turn.

FIRST SHOULDER SHAPING

Next Row (short row): Ch 1, hdc in first 28 (28, 29, 31, 31) sts, turn.

Next Row: Sl st in first 6 sts, hdc across, turn. *22 (22, 23, 25, 25) sts*

Next Row: Ch 1, hdc in first 8 (8, 9, 10, 10) sts. Fasten off.

OPPOSITE SHOULDER SHAPING

Working into last row of Armhole Shaping, skip center 11 (15, 19, 19, 19) sts, join yarn in next st, cont as foll:

Next Row: Ch 1, hdc across, turn.

Next Row (short row): Ch 1, hdc in first 22 (22, 23, 25, 25) sts, turn.

Next Row: Sl st in first 14 (14, 14, 15, 15) hdc, hdc across. Fasten off.

FRONT

With MC, work as for Back through Row 21 (21, 23, 23, 23).

COLOR INSET

Next Row: Ch 1, hdc in first 34 (37, 41, 46, 50) sts, with CC1 (see Mid-Row Col Change, page 79) hdc in next 3 sts, with MC hdc across, turn. *71 (77, 85, 95, 103) sts*

L, 1X Only

Next Row: Ch 1, hdc in first 45 (49) sts, with CC1 hdc in next 5 sts, with MC hdc across, turn.

XS, S, M Only

Next Row: Ch 1, 2 hdc in first st, hdc in next 32 (35, 39) sts, with CC1 hdc in next 5 sts, with MC hdc across ending 2 hdc in last st, turn. *73 (79, 87) sts*

XS, S Only

Next Row: Ch 1, hdc in first 33 (36) sts, with CC1 hdc in next 7 sts, with MC hdc across, turn.

Next Row: Ch 1, 2 hdc in first st, hdc in next 32 (35) sts, with CC1 hdc in next 7 sts, with MC hdc across ending 2 hdc in last st, turn. *75 (81) sts*

All Sizes

Next 2 Rows: Ch 1, hdc in first 33 (36, 40, 44, 48) sts, with CC1 hdc in next 9 (9, 7, 7, 7) sts, with MC hdc across, turn.

Next 15 (17, 19, 19, 21) Rows: Cont shaping as for Back starting with Row 28 AT SAME TIME working 2 more sts

It is actually Elinor who marries Willoughby—in real life, that is. Emma Thompson, who acted the part of Elinor, and Grey Wise, who starred as Willoughby, met on the set of the 1995 movie *Sense and Sensibility* and later married.

with CC1 on next and every 2nd row to start of Back Armhole Shaping. *31 (33, 36, 40, 44) MC; 25 (27, 27, 27, 29) CC1; 31 (33, 36, 40, 44) MC for total 87 (93, 99, 107, 117) sts*

ARMHOLE SHAPING

Rep first 4 rows of Back Armhole Shaping Rows AT SAME TIME working 2 more sts in CC1 every 2nd row. *22 (24, 27, 29, 30) MC; 29 (31, 31, 31, 33) CC1; 22 (24, 27, 29, 30) MC for total 73 (79, 85, 89, 93) sts*

M, L, 1X Only

Next Row: Sl st in first st, hdc in next 25 (27, 28) sts, with CC1 hdc in next 33 (33, 35) sts, with MC hdc across leaving last st unworked, turn. *83 (87, 91) sts*

Next Row: Sl st in first st, hdc in next 24 (26, 27) sts, with CC1 hdc in next 33 (33, 35) sts, with MC hdc across leaving last st unworked, turn. *81 (85, 89) sts*

All Sizes

Cont with Neckline Shaping.

FIRST NECKLINE SHAPING

Next Row: Sl st in first st, hdc in next 21 (23, 23, 24, 26) sts, with CC1 hdc in next 12 (13, 14, 14, 15) sts, turn. *33 (36, 37, 38, 40) sts*

Next Row: Sl st in first 6 sts, hdc in next 6 (7, 8, 8, 9) sts, with MC hdc across leaving last st unworked, turn. *26 (29, 30, 31, 32) sts*

Next Row (dec row): Sl st in first st, hdc in next 19 (21, 21, 22, 22) sts, with CC1 hdc in next 1 (2, 2, 4, 4) st, turn. *20 (23, 23, 26, 26) sts*

Next Row (dec row): Sl st in first 1 (2, 2, 4, 4) st, with MC hdc across, turn. *18 (20, 20, 21, 21) sts*

Next 15 (17, 16, 17, 19) Rows: Cont dec 1 st at neckline edge

every row for 5 (7, 6, 5, 3) times; then dec 1 st every 2nd row for 5 (5, 5, 6, 8) times. *8 (8, 9, 10, 10) sts*
Fasten off.

OPPOSITE NECKLINE SHAPING

Join MC at armhole edge of last row of Armhole Shaping. Rep First Neckline Shaping.

SLEEVE

Make 2
With MC, ch 41 (45, 49, 53, 57).

Row 1: Hdc in 2nd ch from hk (count as hdc) and each ch across, turn. *40 (44, 48, 52, 56) sts*

Rows 2–3: Ch 1, hdc across, turn.

Row 4: Ch 1, 2 hdc in first st, hdc across ending 2 hdc in last st, turn. *42 (46, 50, 54, 58) sts*

Rows 5–6: Ch 1, hdc across, turn.

Row 7: Ch 1, 2 hdc in first st, hdc across ending 2 hdc in last st, turn. *44 (48, 52, 56, 60) sts*

Rows 8–13: Rep last three rows twice. *48 (52, 56, 60, 64) sts*

Row 14: Ch 1, hdc across, turn.

XS, S, M, L Only

Row 15: Ch 1, hdc across, turn. *48 (52, 56, 60) sts*

1X Only

Row 15: Rep Row 4. *66 sts*

All Sizes

Row 16: Ch 1, hdc across, turn.

Row 17: Rep Row 4. *50 (54, 58, 62, 68) sts*

Rows 18–25: Work even with inc (rep Row 4) every 4th row twice. *54 (58, 62, 64, 72) sts*

Rows 26–27: Rep Row 2.

Row 28: Sl st in first 4 sts, hdc across leaving last 4 sts unworked, turn. *46 (50, 54, 58, 64) sts*

Row 29: Sl st in first 2 (2, 2, 3, 3) sts, hdc across leaving last 2 (2, 2, 3, 3) sts unworked, turn. *42 (46, 50, 52, 58) sts*

Row 30: Sl st in first 2 (2, 2, 2, 3) sts, hdc across leaving last 2 (2, 2, 2, 3) sts unworked, turn. *38 (42, 46, 48, 52) sts*

Row 31: Sl st in first 1 (1, 1, 1, 2) st, hdc across leaving last 1 (1, 1, 1, 2) st unworked, turn. *36 (40, 44, 46, 48) sts*

Next 9 (11, 11, 12, 12) Rows: Ch 1, hdc2tog, hdc across to last 2 sts, hdc2tog, turn. *34 (38, 42, 44, 46) sts*

Next 2 Rows: Sl st in first 2 sts, hdc across leaving last 2 sts unworked. *30 (34, 38, 40, 42) sts*

Fasten off.

FINISHING

Steam block to schematic measurements. Sew shoulder and underarm seams, set in sleeves, and sew side seams. With WS facing and MC, work 1 row sl sts around back neckline. With CC1, work 1 row sc around front neckline.

FRONT NECKLINE RUFFLE

With RS facing, join CC1 to right neck shoulder seam. Fpsc (see page 79) down neckline, and along entire length of V shape where MC and CC1 color changes occur, and up neckline; total sts worked must be multiple of 4, turn.

Row 1: Ch 5, dc in same st, *ch 3, sc in next 3 sts, ch 3, (dc, ch 3, dc) in next dc; rep from * across ending last rep (dc, ch 2, dc) in last st, turn.

Row 2: Ch 3, 3 dc in first ch-2 sp, *ch 3, sc in 2nd sc of 3-sc group, ch 3, skip next ch-3 sp, 7 dc in next ch-3 sp; rep from * across ending last rep 4 dc in sp between last dc and tch. Fasten off.

CUFFS

With CC1 and RS of sleeve facing, join yarn to bottom of sleeve at seam.

Rnd 1: Ch 6, dc in same st as base of ch, ch 3, sc in next 3 sts, *ch 3, (dc, ch 3, dc) in next st, ch 3, sc in next 3 sts; rep from * around for 7 (8, 9, 10, 11) times evenly spacing sts (do not work into every foundation ch of sleeve bottom) and ending ch 3, join with sl st in 3rd ch of tch, turn. *24 (27, 30, 33, 36) ch-3 lps*

Rnd 2: Ch 6, sc in 2nd sc of 3-sc group, *ch 3, skip next ch-3 sp, 7 dc in next ch-3 sp, ch 3, sc in 2nd sc of 3-sc group; rep from * around ending last rep in remaining sc of 3-sc group, ch 3, 6 dc in last ch-3 sp, join with sl st in 3rd ch of tch, turn.

Rnd 3: Ch 1, sc in each of next 6 dc, *ch 5, skip next 2 ch-3 sps, sc in each of next 7 dc; rep from * around, join with sl st in first sc, turn.

Rnd 4: *Ch 3, (dc, ch 3, dc) in 3rd ch of next ch-5, ch 3, skip 2 sc, sc in each of next 3 sc; rep from * around, join with sl st in base of tch, turn.

Rnd 5: Ch 1, sc in 2nd sc of 3-sc group, *ch 3, skip next ch-3 sp, 7 dc in next ch-3 sp, ch 3, sc in 2nd sc of 3-sc group; rep from * around ending ch 3, 7 dc in last ch-3 sp between pair of dc sts, ch 3, join with sl st in first sc, turn.

Rnd 6: Ch 3, *sc in each of next 7 dc, ch 5, skip next 2 ch-3 sps; rep from * around, join with sl st in first sc, turn.

Rnd 7: Ch 6, dc in 3rd ch of first ch-5, *ch 3, skip 2 sc, sc in each of next 3 sc, ch 3 (dc ch 3, dc) in 3rd ch of next ch-5;

rep from * around to last 7-sc group, ch 3, skip 2 sc, sc in each of next 3 sc, ch 3, join with sl st in 3rd ch of tch, turn.

Rnd 8: Ch 3, 6 dc in first ch-3 sp, ch 3, sc in 2nd sc of 3-sc group, *ch 3, 7 dc in next ch-3 sp, ch 3, sc in 2nd sc of 3-sc group; rep from * around, ch 3, join with sl st in top of of tch. Fasten off.

Rep rnds 1–8 on opposite sleeve.

VIOLET APPLIQUÉ

Make no less than 6

Rnd 1: With CC1, ch 2, 5 sc in 2nd ch from hk. *5 sc*

Rnd 2: (Sl st, ch 2, 2 dc, ch 2, sl st) in each st around. Fasten off.

LEAF SPRAY APPLIQUÉ

Make at least 1

Beg at bottom of stem, ch 16.

Row 1: For first leaf, 6 tr in 5th ch from hk, turn (7 tr).

Row 2: Ch 3, (dc2tog) twice, dc in next st, leave last st unworked, turn. *4 dc*

Row 3: Ch 1, skip first st, sc2tog, leave last st unworked, do not turn; for tip of leaf, ch 3, sc in 3rd ch from hk; working down side of leaf, ch 1, sl st in top of st at end of Row 1, ch 4, sl st in same ch as 6th tr of Row 1. Do not turn. Do not fasten off.

2nd leaf: Ch 9; rep Rows 1–3 of first leaf; sc in next 4 ch below 2nd leaf. Do not fasten off. Do not turn.

3rd leaf: Ch 5; rep Rows 1–3 of first leaf; sc in each ch across stem. Fasten off.

SINGLE LEAF APPLIQUÉ

Make no less than 2

Ch 7.

Rnd 1: Side 1: Sc in 2nd ch from hk, hdc in next ch, dc in next 3 ch, (2 hdc, ch 2, sc in 2nd ch from hk, 2 hdc in last ch; rotate work; working on opposite side of foundation ch, cont as foll:

Side 2: Dc in next 3 ch, hdc in next ch, sc in last ch. Join with sl st in first sc of rnd. Work tambour crochet (see page 79) up center of leaf by placing yarn at backside of leaf, inserting hk along center of leaf and drawing yarn through lp on hk. Fasten off.

ROSE APPLIQUÉ

Make no less than 3

Ch 2.

Rnd 1: 10 dc in 2nd ch from hk, join with sl st in top of first dc.

Rnd 2: Ch 1, sc in same st, sc in each dc around, join with sl st in first sc.

Rnd 3: Ch 3, skip next st, (sc in next st, ch 2, skip next st) around. join with sc in joining sl st of rnd 2. *5 ch-lps*

Rnd 4: For petals, (sl st, ch 2, 4 dc, ch 2, sl st) in each ch-lp around. *5 petals*

Rnd 5: Working behind petals, ch 1 (sc in back lp of next skipped sc on rnd 2, ch 4) around, join with sl st in first sc. *5 ch-lps*

Rnd 6: For petals (sl st, ch 2, 7 dc, ch 2, sl st) in each ch-lp around. *5 petals*

Fasten off.

APPLIQUÉ FINISHING

Weave in ends. With CC1 and referring to chart (see page 87) hand sew pieces to Front.

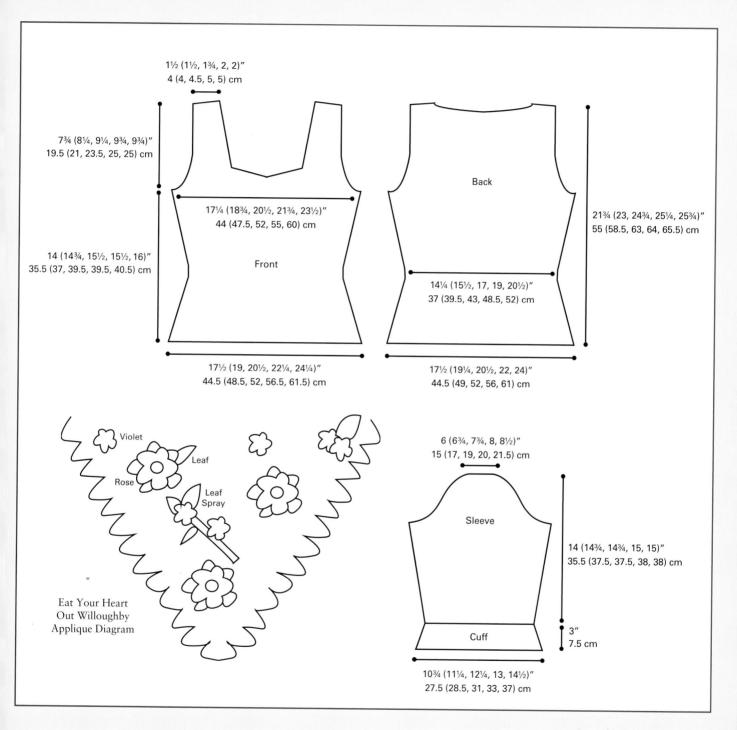

1½ (1½, 1¾, 2, 2)"
4 (4, 4.5, 5, 5) cm

7¾ (8¼, 9¼, 9¾, 9¾)"
19.5 (21, 23.5, 25, 25) cm

17¼ (18¾, 20½, 21¾, 23½)"
44 (47.5, 52, 55, 60) cm

Front

14 (14¾, 15½, 15½, 16)"
35.5 (37, 39.5, 39.5, 40.5) cm

Back

21¾ (23, 24¾, 25¼, 25¾)"
55 (58.5, 63, 64, 65.5) cm

14¼ (15½, 17, 19, 20½)"
37 (39.5, 43, 48.5, 52) cm

17½ (19, 20½, 22¼, 24¼)"
44.5 (48.5, 52, 56.5, 61.5) cm

17½ (19¼, 20½, 22, 24)"
44.5 (49, 52, 56, 61) cm

Violet
Leaf
Rose
Leaf
Spray

Eat Your Heart
Out Willoughby
Applique Diagram

6 (6¾, 7¾, 8, 8½)"
15 (17, 19, 20, 21.5) cm

Sleeve

14 (14¾, 14¾, 15, 15)"
35.5 (37.5, 37.5, 38, 38) cm

3"
7.5 cm

Cuff

10¾ (11¼, 12¼, 13, 14½)"
27.5 (28.5, 31, 33, 37) cm

SKILL LEVEL

MATERIALS

Berroco *Vintage* (50% acrylic, 40% wool, 10% nylon; 217 yds / 198 m; worsted weight #4 medium): #5103 mocha, 3 skeins

G-6 (4 mm) hk or size needed to obtain correct gauge

Stitcher's Kit (see page 187)

GAUGE

12 hdc blo and 12 rows = 4" (10 cm)

FINISHED SIZES

7" x 72" (18 x 183 cm)

STITCH GUIDE

View an online video demonstrating how to create this stitch pattern at: www.stitchscene.com/tutorials

He's a complicated man, an enigma you delight in puzzling over; he's all male, yet can appreciate the finer things. As such, your Mr. Darcy will enjoy the comfort and styling of this warm mocha scarf. A combination of stitch patterns, including cabled crosses, add depth and interest while remaining distinctively masculine—an arrangement sure to please even the most discerning of suitors. Lightweight yet loaded with texture, it's another way for you to wrap yourself around him.

FOUNDATION CROSS DOUBLE CROCHET STITCH (FCross2dc)

Sk next 2 ch, dc in next ch, ch 2, working behind dc just made, dc in first skipped ch.

Note: To cont FCross2dc across row, skip 2 ch as counted from first dc of FCross2dc just worked, and place first dc of next "cross" in next (3rd) ch.

CROSS DOUBLE CROCHET STITCH (Cross2dc)

Sk 3 dc, dc in next dc, ch 2, working behind dc just made, dc in first skipped dc.

Note: To cont Cross2dc across row, skip 2 ch as counted from first dc of Cross2dc just worked and place first dc of next cross in next (3rd) ch.

Note: Ch 1 at beg of row does not count as st throughout.

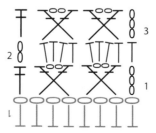

stitch key
o = chain (ch)
⊤ = half double crochet (hdc)
Ŧ = double crochet (dc)

Cross Double Crochet Stitch Pattern Chart

SCARF

Ch 219.

SIDE ONE

Row 1: Hdc in 2nd ch from hk (count as hdc), hdc in next and each ch across, turn. *218 hdc*

Rows 2–11: Ch 2 (count as hdc), hdc blo across, turn. Fasten off.

SIDE TWO

Rotate work. With foundation ch is at top and RS facing join yarn to beg of foundation ch.

Row 1: Ch 3 (count as dc) *FCross2dc (see page 88); rep from * across, ending dc in last ch, turn. *108 crosses*

Row 2: Ch 2 (count as hdc), *3 hdc in ch-2 sp, hdc in next dc; rep from * across ending hdc in top of tch, turn.

Row 3: Ch 3 (count as dc), *Cross2dc (see page 88); rep from * across ending dc in top of tch, turn.

Row 4: Rep Row 2.

Rows 5–8: Rep Rows 3 and 4 twice.

Row 9: Rep Row 3. Fasten off.

FINISHING

Weave in ends. Steam block.

Which characters said these swoon-worthy lines?

1. "I was simple enough to think that . . . there could be no danger in my being with you. I told myself it was only friendship . . . I did not know how far I was got."

2. "I have loved none but you."

3. "For half an hour—for ten minutes—I entreat you to stay."

4. "In vain I have struggled . . . my feelings will not be repressed. You must allow me to tell you how ardently I admire and love you."

5. "And now nothing remains for me but to assure you . . . of the violence of my affections."

6. "For you alone I think and plan."

7. "I have thought only of you."

8. "But you have more good-nature . . . and it is not only good-nature, but you have so much—so much of everything; and then you have such—upon my soul, I do not know anybody like you."

9. "You are always with me."

10. "You pierce my soul. I am half agony, half hope."

11. "You are too good."

12. "If I loved you less, I might be able to talk about it more."

13. "My real purpose was to see you, and to judge, if I could, whether I might ever hope to make you love me."

Check your results on page 203.

SKILL LEVEL

MATERIALS

TilliTomas *Voile de la mer* (70% silk, 30% seacell; 290 yds/265 m; laceweight #0 lace): ruby wine 1 skein

B-1 (2.25 mm) hk or size needed to obtain correct gauge

Black seed 6/0 beads

Adjustable hairpin lace loom

10 x 3 mm torpedo clasp

¾" (19 mm) cross pendant (optional)

Stitcher's Kit (see page 187)

GAUGE

28 lps = 4" (10 cm) blocked with sc edging; 19 lps = 4" (10 cm) blocked, without edging, worked on hairpin loom adjusted to 1½" (4 cm).

Note: Measure lps on both sides of strip to determine gauge. Hairpin lace stretches considerably during blocking; it is essential to measure gauge after blocking.

FINISHED SIZES

Custom-sized to neck measurement. Instructions for finished edge are given with twisted edge instructions in parentheses.

STITCH GUIDE

View an online video demonstrating how to create this stitch pattern at: www.stitchscene.com/tutorials

You won't go unnoticed wearing this choker-style necklace. A convertible design, it can be made and worn in several ways: a straight traditional manner with refined edging, or twisted for a modern-day look. You decide. Add a cross like the one Fanny received from her brother or another charm of your choice from the Austen era: a cameo, perhaps? No matter what style you choose, demure or bold, you'll fall in love with this design every time you adorn yourself with its unique beauty.

BEAD AND LOOP COUNT

Measure where you would like the necklace to be positioned when worn. Subtract 1" (2.5 cm). Divide that number by 4, then multiply by 28 (19) for number of loops needed. Thread same number of beads on yarn.

Set loom width at 1½" (4 cm) wide. Leaving 6" (15 cm) tail, work basic hairpin lace stitch drawing through a bead with last yo of each sc, then draw through to complete st. Cont drawing through beads into center of each sc to desired lp number.

Fasten off leaving 6" (15 cm) inch tail. Remove strip from loom.

FINISHING
CHOKER WITH EDGING ONLY

Join yarn to end loop,*insert hk from back of loop to front to work sc; rep from * across strip.

Fasten off.

Rep for other side of strip.

BOTH CHOKERS

Attach torpedo clasp to yarn tails at strip ends. Thread in row ends. Block necklace to neck circumference measurement minus 1″ (2.5 cm) allowing for screw clasp. Sew on pendant (optional).

During the course of *Emma*, how many men does Harriet Smith fall in love with?

Find out on page 203.

JANE BENNET SKIRT

SKILL LEVEL

MATERIALS

Cascade *Venezia Worsted* (70% merino wool, 30% silk; 218 yds/200 m; dk weight #3 light): #172 bluebell (MC) 7 (7, 8, 9, 10, 11) skeins; #110 ivory (CC1) 3 (3, 3, 4, 4, 5) skeins

E-4 (3.5 mm) hk or size needed to obtain correct gauge

¾" (19 mm) wide elastic matching length to body waist circumference + 1" (2.5 cm)

5" (13 cm) satin bow made with 1½" (4 cm) wide ribbon

Stitcher's Kit (see page 187)

GAUGE

17 sc and 20 rows = 4" (10 cm) hung gauge (see page 188)

FINISHED SIZES

XS (S, M, L, 1X, 2X) full hip measurement 37 (40, 43, 46, 50, 55)"/94 (101.5, 109, 117, 127, 140) cm

Note: Skirt waist must be large enough to pull over hips. Elastic will gather excess fabric for custom fit at waist.

STITCH GUIDE

View an online video demonstrating how to create this stitch pattern at: www.stitchscene.com/tutorials

*G*arner the attention Jane Bennet received from Mr. Bingley in this delightful A-line skirt. The ruffles in this design give the skirt unexpected panache when viewed from behind. A simple elastisized waist makes for a comfortable fit. Stitch the skirt in demure colors to showcase your irresistible femininity, go for a bolder combination like black with cream for an edgier twist, or simply leave off the ruffle altogether. Worked from the top down, it can be lengthened or shortened as desired, providing a versatility that showcases your individual style.

FRONT POST SINGLE CROCHET STITCH (fpsc)

Insert hk around post of specified stitch (from front to back and then back to front) in previous row, work as for single crochet.

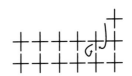

Front post single crochet stitch

TAMBOUR CROCHET STITCHING

Start chain on crocheted fabric surface with yarn beneath finished work at beg of desired design line. Insert hk through fabric, yo and draw through lp. *Working along design line, insert hk through crocheted fabric slightly forward from last position, yo and draw lp

through fabric and through lp on hk–surface ch made. Rep
from * along design line. At end of line cut working yarn, remove hk from last lp, place hk underneath fabric and
draw through lp. Draw yarn tail through lp to fasten off on WS.

Note: Ch 1 and/or sl st(s) at beg of row do not count as st(s)
throughout.

WAIST CASING

With MC, ch 141 (153, 161, 173, 189, 209).

Row 1: Sc in 2nd ch from hk and each ch across, turn.
140 (152, 160, 172, 188, 208) sts

Row 2: Ch 1, sc in each st across, turn.

Row 3: Rep Row 2.

Row 4: Ch 1, sc in each st across; being careful not to twist
work, join with sl st in first st, turn. Do not fasten off.

FRONT AND BACK

Note: One piece worked in continuous rnds. Pm to note beg
of each rnd being sure to move marker up with each new rnd.

Rnd 1: Ch 1, sc in each st around, do not turn.

Rnd 2: Sc in each st around.

Next 2 (2, 1, 1, 1, 1) Rnds: Rep Rnd 2.

Pm in foll sts:

    XS: 35, 70, 105;

    S: 38, 76, 114;

    M: 40, 80, 120;

    L: 43, 86, 129;

    1X: 47, 94, 141;

    2X: 52, 104, 156.

Next Rnd (inc rnd): Sc in each st around working 2 sc in each

How many sisters did Mr. Bingley bring to Netherfield
and how many attended the assembly with him?

Find out on page 203.

marked st (including beg-of-rnd marker).
144 (156, 164, 176, 192, 212) sts

Next 5 (5, 3, 3, 3, 3) Rnds: Rep Rnd 2.

Next Rnd: Rep inc rnd. *148 (160, 168, 180, 196, 216) sts*

Next 6 (12, 12, 8, 4, 10) Rnds: Work even with inc every 6th (6th, 6th, 4th, 4th, 5th) rnd for 1 (2, 2, 2, 1, 2) time. *152 (168, 176, 188, 200, 224) sts*

Next 7 (7, 7, 24, 5, 14) Rnds: Work even with inc every 7th (7th, 7th, 8th, 5th, 7th) rnd for 1 (1, 1, 3, 1, 2) time. *156 (172, 180, 200, 204, 232) sts*

Next 30 (20, 8, 9, 21, 27) Rnds: Work even with inc every 10th (10th, 8th, 9th, 7th, 9th) rnd for 3 (2, 1, 1, 3, 3) times. *168 (180, 184, 204, 216, 244) sts*

Next 24 (48, 10, 33, 9, 48) Rnds: Work even with inc every 12th (12th, 10th, 11th, 9th, 12th) rnd for 2 (4, 1, 3, 1, 4) times. *176 (196, 188, 216, 220, 260) sts*

Next 14 (0, 48, 13, 60, 0) Rnds: Work even with inc every 14th (0, 12th, 13th, 12th, 0) rnd for 1 (0, 4, 1, 5, 0) time. *180 (196, 204, 220, 240, 260) sts*

Next 14 (12, 21, 21, 17, 19) Rnds: Rep Rnd 2.

Remove markers.

Fasten off.

RUFFLES

Let skirt hang overnight to ensure desired length before weaving in ends and beg ruffle tiers.

FIRST TIER

This tier is closest to hem and worked down, toward hem. Position skirt with waist closest and hem farthest away. With RS facing and CC1 join yarn to 5th row from bottom, directly above position of last fasten off, leaving 8" (20 cm) tail for securing side edges of ruffle to skirt.

Row 1: Working around posts of sts in same rnd as join, fpsc (see page 95) around next 58 sts, turn.

Row 2: Ch 1, 2 sc in each fpsc, turn. *116 sts*

Row 3: Ch 1, 2 sc in first sc, sc across ending 2 sc in last sc, turn. *118 sts*

Rows 4–7: Rep Row 3. *126 sts*

Fasten off leaving 8" (20 cm) tail. Tuck under ruffle sides. Sew first 4 rows of ruffle to skirt.

TIERS 2–9

Again position skirt with waist closest and hem farthest away. Join CC1 to 5th row above top of ruffle just made, cont as foll:

Second Tier: Join 3 sts to left of previous ruffle; work 52 fpsc for Row 1; rep Rows 2–7 of First Tier. *114 sts*

Third Tier: Join 4 sts to left of previous ruffle; work 44 fpsc for Row 1; rep Rows 2–7 of First Tier. *98 sts*

Fourth Tier: Join 3 sts to left of previous ruffle; work 38 fpsc for Row 1; rep Rows 2–7 of First Tier. *86 sts*

Fifth Tier: Join 3 sts to left of previous ruffle; work 32 fpsc for Row 1; rep Rows 2–7 of First Tier. *74 sts*

Sixth Tier: Join 2 sts to left of previous ruffle; work 28 fpsc for Row 1; rep Rows 2–7 of First Tier. *66 sts*

Seventh Tier: Join 2 sts to left of previous ruffle; work 24 fpsc for Row 1; rep Rows 2–7 of First Tier. *58 sts*

Eighth Tier: Join 2 sts to left of previous ruffle; work 20 fpsc for Row 1; rep Rows 2–7 of First Tier. *50 sts*

Ninth Tier: Join 2 sts to left of previous ruffle; work 16 fpsc for Row 1; rep Rows 2–7 of First Tier. *42 sts*

FINISHING

Work 1 row of tambour crochet (see page 95) over intersection of Ninth Tier and skirt body. Weave in ends. Make elastic casing (see page 196). Steam block, pinning ruffled edges neatly. Sew satin bow to top of ruffles.

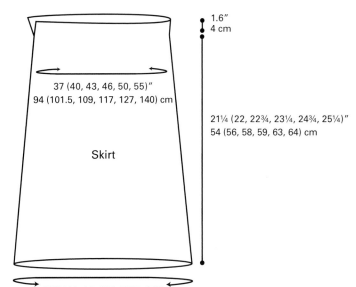

1.6"
4 cm

37 (40, 43, 46, 50, 55)"
94 (101.5, 109, 117, 127, 140) cm

21¼ (22, 22¾, 23¼, 24¾, 25¼)"
54 (56, 58, 59, 63, 64) cm

Skirt

42¼ (46, 48, 51¾, 56½, 61)"
107.5 (117, 122, 133.5, 143.5, 155) cm

CHAPTER 4

Better with Age: Timeless Designs to Cherish Always

> "It sometimes happens that a woman
>
> is handsomer at twenty-nine
>
> than she was ten years before."
>
> —*Persuasion*

"Back and forth and forth and back. I wish she would just sit either at her needlework or at her desk," spoke Elinor. "Marianne's unpredictable behavior wears on my nerves often enough and I simply cannot abide when Miss Austen does the same."

"Yes. It is really quite impossible to relax when she carries on so," replied Fanny.

Upon recognizing that the last half hour of work on her shawl would need to be restitched, her tension having gone too tight, Elinor sighed with frustration and dropped her work into the basket near her feet, gently flexing her hands.

When Jane exchanged her pen for needle once again, Emma spoke up. "Needlework is so very inspiring is it not, Miss Austen?" She picked up a sock in need of mending, looked at it queerly, and then passed it over to Fanny.

"Quite right, Emma," replied Miss Austen, "You really should try more of it." Miss Austen worked steadily for several minutes, her stitches neat and precise, before her face and hand froze momentarily. She hurried to her desk, dipped her pen, and wrote. A moment later she returned to the settee.

Elinor looked at Elizabeth. "Your turn," I heard her mouth softly.

"An afternoon of diligent stitching deserves some entertainment, wouldn't you agree, Miss Austen? Words seem to be in your favor today. Care to share with us what has been able to tempt you away from your dearest brother's shirts?"

"You shall all find out soon enough."

"It is really quite naughty of you not to fill us in," joined in Marianne. "It is our life and only quite right for us to be privy to it. "

"Perhaps," said Miss Austen. "But today's writing is often tomorrow's rubbish. Also, I find there is some measure of ill-discipline within me that takes delight in springing surprises on each of you. Reactions are never quite so honest as when each of you learns the details for the first time."

"At your age, Miss Austen, one would hope you would be less childish," Marianne scoffed.

"My age?" Miss Austen inquired, brows arched.

"Marianne, I am near her age," Anne noted. "You make it positively sound as if we are in our dotage."

"A woman of seven and twenty can never hope to feel or inspire affection again," quipped Marianne. "And

I would die without either."

Again Miss Austen paused in her stitching. "You are quite wrong Marianne. Some of us may by circumstances of our choice or not, remain unmarried, but affection is not given by the opposite sex alone. Consider Cassandra and me." Miss Austen picked up her hook and resumed the flower she was stitching. "Anne, despite being the age you speak of, still feels affection for a certain gentlemen and I shall enjoy showing you, Marianne, that even at our advanced age, we can inspire affection in a man as well."

"Well, you are the authoress so of course you can make it so," Marianne replied. "But let us make it even more interesting and see how you go about doing so in the man Anne slighted."

SKILL LEVEL

MATERIALS

Nashua Handknits *Julia* (50% wool, 25% alpaca, 25% mohair; 93 yds/ 85 m; worsted weight #4 medium): #5185 spring green (MC) 10 (10, 11, 12, 13) skeins, #6086 velvet moss (CC1) 2 skeins.

G-6 (4 mm) hk or size needed to obtain correct gauge

F-5 (3.75 mm) hk or size needed to obtain correct gauge

Stitcher's Kit (see page 187)

GAUGE

13 sc and 16 rows = 4" (10 cm)

FINISHED SIZES

XS (S, M, L, 1X) has bust circumference of 35 (38¾, 41, 45, 47¼)"/89 (98.5, 104, 114, 120) cm

STITCH GUIDE

View an online video demonstrating how to create this stitch pattern at: www.stitchscene.com/tutorials

No Regency wardrobe would be complete without the cropped Spencer jacket. Originally designed for men, it is said to be named for the Earl of Spencer, who favored such coats; but women know a good design when they see it. Though the style may be borrowed from him, the shape is distinctly hers, making this coat as fashionable now as it was then. Worked in a simple stitch to complement the jacket's simple lines, you can easily crochet this while watching your favorite Austen movies.

SINGLE CROCHET DECREASE (sc2tog)

Insert hk in st, yo and draw through st, insert hk in next st, yo and draw through st, yo and draw through all 3 lps on hk.

LONG SINGLE CROCHET (long sc)

Insert hk in designated st, draw through long lp, keeping lp taut but not tight yo and draw through both lps on hk.

Note: Ch 1 and/or sl st(s) at beg of rows do not count as st(s) throughout.

LEFT FRONT

Make 2

With MC, ch 26 (28, 30, 33, 35) sts.

Row 1 (RS): Sc in 2nd ch from hk and each ch across, turn. *25 (27, 29, 32, 34) sts*

Row 2: Ch 1, sc across, turn.

Row 3: Ch 1, 2 sc in first st—inc made at side seam, sc across, turn. *26 (28, 30, 33, 35) sts*

Next 22 (20, 20, 20, 20) Rows: Work in sc with inc at side seam every 5th (4th, 4th, 4th, 4th) row twice, then every 4th (3rd, 3rd, 3rd, 3rd) row for 3 (4, 4, 4, 4)

times. *31 (34, 36, 39, 41) sts*

Next 2 (4, 4, 2, 2) Rows: Rep Row 2.

ARMHOLE SHAPING

Row 28 (28, 28, 26, 26): Ch 1, sc across leaving last 3 sts unworked—dec made at armhole, turn. *28 (31, 33, 36, 38) sts*

Row 29 (29, 29, 27, 27): Sl st in first 2 sts, sc across, turn. *26 (29, 31, 34, 36) sts*

Row 30 (30, 30, 28, 28): Ch 1, sc across leaving last 0 (0, 2, 2, 2) st unworked, turn. *26 (29, 29, 32, 34) sts*

L, 1X Only

Row 29 (dec row): Ch 1, sc2tog (see page 102), sc across, turn. *(31, 33) sts*

Row 30: Ch 1, sc across to last 2 sts, sc2tog, turn. *(30, 32) sts*

Row 31: Rep dec row. *(29, 31) sts*

Row 32: Ch 1, sc across, turn.

FIRST SHOULDER SHAPING

Row 31 (31, 31, 33, 33) (short row): Ch 1, sc (sc2tog, sc2tog, sc2tog, sc2tog) in first st(s), sc across leaving last 7 sts unworked—dec made for neckline, turn. *19 (21, 21, 21, 23) sts*

Next 24 (24, 24, 28, 28) Rows: Work in sc AT SAME TIME dec 1 st at neckline every 6th (4th, 4th, 6th, 5th) row for 4 (6, 6, 4, 4) times, then every 0 (0, 0, 2nd, 2nd) row for 0 (0, 0, 2, 4) times. *15 sts*

PM at neckline edge of Row 39 (39, 39, 41, 41)—7th row of group of rows just worked.

Next 1 (3, 5, 1, 3) Rows: Ch 1, sc across, turn.

Row 57 (59, 61, 63, 65): Sl st in first 0 (1, 2, 2, 4) sts, sc across, turn. *15 (14, 13, 13, 11) sts*

Next Row (short row): Ch 1, sc in first 7 (7, 7, 8, 9) sts, turn.

Next Row: Sl st in first 2 (2, 2, 2, 3) sts, sc across. *5 (5, 5, 6, 6) sts*

Fasten off. Do not remove marker.

RIGHT FRONT

With MC, ch 26 (28, 30, 33, 35) sts.

Row 1 (RS): Sc in 2nd ch from hk and each ch across, turn. *25 (27, 29, 32, 34) sts*

Row 2: Ch 1, sc across, turn.

Row 3: Ch 1, sc across ending 2 sc in last sc—inc made at side seam, turn. *26 (28, 30, 33, 35) sts*

Next 4 Rows: Ch 1, sc across, turn.

Row 8 (WS): Ch 1, 2 sc in first st—inc made, sc across to last 3 sts, ch 2, skip 2 sc, sc in last sc, turn—buttonhole started. *27 (29, 31, 34, 36) sts*

Row 9: Ch 1, sc in first sc, 2 sc in ch-lp, sc in next sc—buttonhole finished, sc across.

Next 6 (6, 6, 8, 8) Rows: Work in sc across with inc at side seam every 3rd (3rd, 3rd, 4th, 4th) row. *29 (31, 33, 36, 38) sts*

XS, S, M Only

Row 16: Ch 1, sc across, turn.

Row 17: Ch 1, sc in first st, ch 2, skip 2 sc, sc in next sc—buttonhole started, sc across, turn.

Row 18: Ch 1, work 1 (2, 2) sc in first st, sc across to ch-lp, 2 sc in ch-lp, sc in next sc—buttonhole finished, turn. *(29, 32, 34) sts*

L, XL Only

Rows 18–19: Rep Rows 8–9—buttonhole made. *(37, 39) sts*

All Sizes

Next 7 (7, 7, 6, 6) Rows: Work in sc with inc at side seam every 4th (4th, 4th, 3rd, 3rd) row for 1 (1, 1, 2, 2,) time; then work even for 3 (3, 3, 0, 0) rows. *30 (33, 35, 39, 41) sts*

XS, S, M only

Next 2 Rows: Rep Rows 8–9—buttonhole made. *31 (34, 36) sts*

ARMHOLE SHAPING

XS, S, M Only

Row 28: Sl st in first 3 sts, sc across, turn. *28 (31, 33) sts*

Row 29: Ch 1, sc across leaving last 2 sts unworked. *26 (29, 31) sts*

Row 30 (short row): Sl first 0 (0, 2) st, sc across leaving last 7 sts unworked—dec made at neckline, turn. *19 (22, 22) sts*

L, XL Only

Row 26: Sl st in first 3 sts, sc across, turn. *(36, 38) sts*

Row 27: Ch 1, sc in first st, ch 2, skip 2 sc, sc in next sc—buttonhole started, sc across leaving last 2 sts unworked, turn. *(34, 36) sts*

Row 28: Sl st in first 2 sts, sc across to ch-lp, 2 sc in ch-lp, sc in next sc—buttonhole finished. *(32, 34) sts*

Next 3 Rows: Work in sc with dec at side seam every row. *(29, 31) sts*

Row 32 (short row): Ch 1, sc across leaving last 7 sts unworked. *(22, 24) sts*

All Sizes

Row 31 (31, 31, 33, 33): Ch 1, sc across leaving last 0 (1, 1, 1, 1) sts unworked. *19 (21, 21, 21, 23) sts*

Next 24 (24, 24, 28, 28) Rows: Work in sc across AT SAME TIME dec 1 st at neckline every 6th (4th, 4th, 6th, 5th) row for 4 (6, 6, 4, 4) times, then every 0 (0, 0, 2nd, 2nd) row for 0 (0, 0, 2, 4) times. *15 sts*

James W. Usher 1916

Something Borrowed

The green and white striped spencer with scalloped sleeves worn by Jane Bennet in the 1995 version of *Pride and Prejudice* is the same one worn by Anne Elliot in the 2007 remake of *Persuasion*.

The brown velvet gown Marianne Dashwood wears while packing up books in Norland's library in the 2008 remake of *Sense and Sensibility*, is the same gown Elizabeth Bennet, played by Keira Knightly in 1995, wore while visiting Pemberley.

PM at neckline edge of Row 39 (39, 39, 41, 41)—7th row of group of rows just worked.

Next 2 (4, 6, 1, 3) Rows: Ch 1, sc across, turn.

Next Row: Ch 1, sc across leaving last 0 (1, 2, 2, 4) sts unworked turn. *15 (14, 13, 11, 11) sts*

Next Row: Sl st in first 8 (7, 6, 4, 2) sts, sc across, turn. *7 (7, 7, 8, 9) sts*

Next Row: Ch 1, sc across leaving last 2 (2, 2, 2, 3) sts unworked. *5 (5, 5, 6, 6) sts*

Fasten off. Do not remove marker.

BACK

With MC, ch 45 (49, 53, 59, 63).

Row 1: Sc in 2nd ch from hk and in each ch across, turn. *44 (48, 52, 58, 62) sts*

Row 2: Ch 1, sc across, turn.

Row 3 (inc row): Ch 1, 2 sc in first st, sc across ending 2 sc in last st, turn. *46 (50, 54, 60, 64) sts*

Next 14 (18, 18, 18, 18) Rows: Work in sc with inc row every 5th row twice, then every 4th row for 1 (2, 2, 2, 2) time. *52 (58, 62, 68, 72) sts*

Next 10 (6, 6, 4, 4) Rows: Ch 1, sc in first and each st across, turn.

ARMHOLE SHAPING

Row 28 (28, 28, 26, 26): Sl st in first 3 sts, sc across leaving last 3 sts unworked, turn. *46 (52, 56, 62, 66) sts*

Next Row: Sl st in first 2 sts, sc across leaving last 2 sts unworked, turn. *42 (48, 52, 58, 62) sts*

Next 4 Rows: Work in sc AT SAME TIME dec 0 (0, 1, 2, 2) st each side once, 0 (0, 0, 1, 1) st each side once; work even once; then dec 0 (0, 0, 0, 1) st each side once. *42 (48, 50, 52, 54) sts*

Next 23 (25, 27, 31, 33) Rows: Ch 1, sc in each st across, turn.

FIRST SHOULDER SHAPING

Row 57 (59, 61, 63, 65) (short row): Ch 1, sc in first 16 (15, 13, 12, 11) sts, turn.

Next Row (short row): Ch 1, sc in first 7 (7, 7, 8, 9) sts, turn.

Next Row: Sl st in first 2 (2, 2, 2, 3) sts, sc in each st across. *5 (5, 5, 6, 6) sts*

Fasten off.

OPPOSITE SHOULDER SHAPING

Join MC to outer edge of opposite armhole and rep First Shoulder Shaping.

Fasten off.

"My kerseymere spencer is quite the comfort of our evening walks"

—Jane in letter dated June 1808

SLEEVE

Make 2

With MC, ch 27 (29, 31, 33, 33).

Row 1: Sc in 2nd ch from hk and in each ch across, turn. *26 (28, 30, 32, 32) sts*

Rows 2–3: Ch 1, sc in each st across, turn.

Row 4 (inc row): Ch 1, 2 sc in first st, sc in each st across ending 2 sc in last st, turn. *28 (30, 32, 34, 34) sts*

Next 64 (64, 64, 71, 69): Work in sc with inc row every 8th (8th, 8th, 8th, 6th) row for 8 times, then every 7th row for 0 (0, 0, 1, 3) time. *44 (46, 48, 52, 56) sts*

Next 2 (2, 2, 0, 2) Rows: Ch 1, sc in each st across, turn.

CAP SHAPING

Next Row: Sl st in first 3 sc, sc in each st across leaving last 3 sc unworked, turn. *38 (40, 42, 46, 50) sts*

Next 2 Rows: Sl st in first 2 sts, sc in each st across leaving last 2 sc unworked, turn. *30 (32, 34, 38, 42) sts*

Next 8 (1, 1, 1, 14) Row: Ch 1, sc2tog, sc in each st across ending sc2tog, turn. *14 (30, 32, 36, 14) sts*

S, M, L Only

Next Row: Ch 1, sc across, turn.

Next 8 (2, 3) Rows: Ch 1, sc2tog, sc in each st across ending sc2tog, turn. *14 (28, 30) sts*

M, L Only

Next Row: Ch 1, sc in each st across, turn.

Next (7, 8) Rows: Ch 1, sc2tog, sc in each st across ending sc2tog, turn. *14 sts*

Fasten off.

FINISHING

Weave in ends. Steam block to schematic measurements. Sew shoulder and underarm seams. Set in sleeves. Sew side seams.

COLLAR

With CC1 and RS facing, join yarn at marker on Left Front.

Row 1: Ch 1, work 64 (70, 74, 78, 82) evenly spaced sc around neckline to marker on Right Front. Remove markers.

Row 2: Ch 1, 2 sc in first st, sc across working 3 sts at each shoulder seam and pm in center st of each inc-group and ending 2 sc in last sc, turn. *6 sts inc*

Rows 3–6: Ch 1, 2 sc in first st, sc across working 3 sts in each marked st (move marker up to 2nd st of inc just made) and 2 sc in last sc, turn. *6 sts inc*

Rows 7–8: Ch 1, sc2tog, sc across working 3 sc in each marked st, sc last 2 sts tog, turn. *2 sts inc*

Row 9 (RS, short row): Ch 1, sc2tog, sc in first 10 sts, turn. *11 sts*

Row 10: Ch 1, sc2tog, sc across ending sc2tog, turn. *9 sts*

Row 11: Ch 1, sc2tog, sc across, turn. *8 sts*

Rows 12–14: Rep Rows 10 and 11; then Row 10. *3 sts*

Fasten off.

At opposite side of collar join yarn to 12th st from beg.

Rep Rows 9–14.

With RS facing sl st around outer edge of collar.

BUTTON

With smaller hk, CC1, and starting with 12" (30.5 cm) long tail, ch 3, join with sl st in first ch.

Rnd 1: Ch 1, 8 sc in ring, join with st in first ch. *8 sc*

Rnd 2: Ch 1, (sc in next st, 2 sc in next st) 4 times, join with sl st in first ch; pull yarn tail through center of ring to WS. *12 sc*

Rnd 3: Ch 1, 16 long sc (see page 102) through center of ring and around sts in Rnds 2 and 3, join with sl st in first ch.

Rnd 4: Ch 1, sc in every other st, join with sl st in first ch. *8 sc*

Fasten off leaving 12" (30.5 cm) tail..

With tail and tapestry needle whip st (see page 199) in flo of each Rnd 4 st. Pull yarn tightly toward button's center on WS. Knot yarn tails tog.

Make 2 more buttons.

Sew buttons to left front 1" (2.5 cm) from edge.

The Spencer Jacket is not the only thing a lady has borrowed from a lord. The 7th Earl of Cardigan is said to have favored a long sleeve, worsted military jacket with a fur or braided center, which later came to be knit at home with a button band front and referred to as a cardigan. Lord Raglan, after losing an arm in the Crimean War, had his tailor design a jacket with a diagonal sleeve to make dressing easier. It is known as the raglan sleeve.

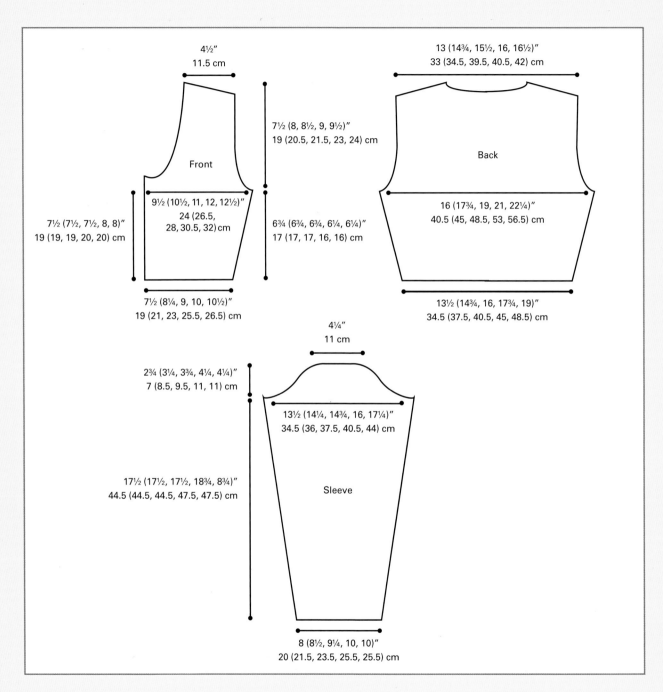

4½"
11.5 cm

13 (14¾, 15½, 16, 16½)"
33 (34.5, 39.5, 40.5, 42) cm

7½ (8, 8½, 9, 9½)"
19 (20.5, 21.5, 23, 24) cm

Front

Back

9½ (10½, 11, 12, 12½)"
24 (26.5, 28, 30.5, 32) cm

7½ (7½, 7½, 8, 8)"
19 (19, 19, 20, 20) cm

6¾ (6¾, 6¾, 6¼, 6¼)"
17 (17, 17, 16, 16) cm

16 (17¾, 19, 21, 22¼)"
40.5 (45, 48.5, 53, 56.5) cm

7½ (8¼, 9, 10, 10½)"
19 (21, 23, 25.5, 26.5) cm

13½ (14¾, 16, 17¾, 19)"
34.5 (37.5, 40.5, 45, 48.5) cm

4¼"
11 cm

2¾ (3¼, 3¾, 4¼, 4¼)"
7 (8.5, 9.5, 11, 11) cm

13½ (14¼, 14¾, 16, 17¼)"
34.5 (36, 37.5, 40.5, 44) cm

17½ (17½, 17½, 18¾, 8¾)"
44.5 (44.5, 44.5, 47.5, 47.5) cm

Sleeve

8 (8½, 9¼, 10, 10)"
20 (21.5, 23.5, 25.5, 25.5) cm

SKILL LEVEL

MATERIALS

Cascade *Heritage*, (75% merino superwash, 25% nylon; 437 yds/400 m; fingering weight #1 superfine): #5602, 4 (6, 8) skeins

D-3 (3.25 mm) hk or size needed to obtain correct gauge

Stitcher's Kit (see page 187)

GAUGE

First 3 rows of patt (see page 116) = 4" (10 cm) diameter, blocked

FINISHED SIZES

S (M, L) fits XS through 2X with bust of 28–35 (36–47, 48–55)"/71–89 (91.5–119, 122–140) cm. This garment has a very forgiving fit, which is ideal for a fuller figure. On a less voluptuous body the hemline is lower on the body. Garment can be closed with an accessory, as shown (see page 113), or left open.

STITCH GUIDE

View an online video demonstrating how to create this stitch pattern at: www.stitchscene.com/tutorials

omantic ruffles and a waterfall edge compose this quixotic cardigan. Worked entirely in the round, this seamless design is easy to recreate using an array of uncomplicated stitches. The dramatic fit and flare design pairs easily with a skirt or a pair of jeans. Stitch in a bright coquelicot (poppy red) or jonquil (daffodil yellow) color for a modern allure that will take you from tea party to first date.

CLUSTER STITCH

*Yo, insert hk in specified st, yo and draw through stitch, yo and draw through 2 lps on hk; rep from * two more times, yo and draw through all 4 lps on hk.

PICOT STITCH

Ch 3, sl st in 3rd ch from hk.

FRONTS AND BACK

Notes: Worked entirely in the round. Pm to note beg of each rnd being sure to move marker up with each new rnd.

Ch 6, join with sl st in first ch.

Rnd 1: Ch 4 (count as dc and ch 1), (dc, ch 1) 17 times, join with sl in 3rd ch of tch, turn. *18 ch-1 sps*

Rnd 2: Ch 3 (count as dc), *yo, insert hk in stitch, yo and draw through stitch, yo and draw through 2 lps on the hk; rep from * once, insert hk in last ch of Rnd 1, yo and draw through 3 lps on hk—partial cluster st made), Ch 2, (cluster, ch 3) in each ch-1 sp around, join with sl st in top of tch, turn. *17 cluster sts (partial cluster sts not counted throughout)*

Rnd 3: Ch 1 (do not count as st), (sc, ch 3, sl st in 3rd ch from hk—picot made, sc) in first ch-3 sp, ch 3, *(sc, picot, sc) in next ch-3 sp, ch 3; rep from * around, join with sl st in first sc, turn. *18 picots*

Rnd 4: Ch 3, dc in first ch-3 sp, ch 3; (2 dc, ch 3) in each ch-3 sp around, join with sl st in top of tch, turn. *18 ch-3 sps*

Rnd 5: Ch 3, (dc, ch 1, 2 dc) in first ch-3 sp, ch 2, *(2 dc, ch 1, 2 dc, ch 2) in each ch-3 sp around, ch 2, join with sl st in top of tch, turn.

Rnd 6: Ch 6 (counts as dc and ch-3 sp), *(2 dc, ch 1, 2 dc, ch 3) in each ch-1 sp around ending (2 dc, ch 1, 1 dc) in last ch-1 sp, join with sl in 3rd ch of tch, turn.

Rnd 7: Ch 3, (dc, ch 1, 2 dc) in first ch-1 sp, ch 3, work 1 sc around first Rnd 6 ch-3 sp and Rnd 5 ch-2 sp, ch 3, *(2 dc, ch 1, 2 dc) in next ch-1 sp, ch 3, work 1 sc around next Rnd 6 ch-3 sp and Rnd 5 ch-2 sp, ch 3; rep from * around, join with sl st in top of tch.

Rnd 8: Ch 6 (count as dc and ch-3 sp), dc in first sc, *ch 3 (dc, ch 1, dc) in next ch-1 sp, ch 3, dc in next sc; rep from * around to last ch-1 sp, (dc, ch 1, dc) in last ch-1 sp, join with sl st in 3rd ch of tch, turn. *36 ch-3 sps*

Rnd 9: Ch 1 (do not count as st), (sc, picot, sc) in first ch-1 sp, skip next dc, ch 3, (sc, picot, sc) in next dc, ch 3, *(sc, picot, sc) in next ch-1 sp, skip next dc, ch 3, (sc, picot, sc) in next dc, ch 3; rep from * around, join with sl st in first sc, turn.

Next 6 (12, 18) Rnds: Rep Rnds 4–9 for 1 (2, 3) time. *72 (144, 288) ch-3 sps*

ARMHOLE SHAPING

Rnd 16 (22, 28): Ch 3 (count as dc), dc in first ch-3 sp, ch 3; *2 dc in next ch-3 sp, ch 3; rep from * for 12 (30, 65) times more, ch 30 (35, 40), skip 10 (11, 12) picots, *2 dc in next ch-3 sp, ch 3; rep from * 26 (61, 132) times more, ch 30 (35, 40), skip 10 (11, 12) picots, **2 dc in next ch-3 sp, ch 3; rep from ** around join with sl st in first dc, turn. *52 (122, 264) ch-3 sps*

Rnd 17 (23, 29): Part 1: Ch 3 (count as dc), *(dc, ch 1, 2 dc) in first ch-3 sp, ch 2, *(2 dc, ch 1, 2 dc) in next ch-3 sp, ch 2; rep from * around AT SAME TIME working (2 dc, ch 1, 2 dc, ch 2), for 11 (12, 13) times over each armhole ch and ending (2 dc, ch 1, dc) in last ch-3 sp, ch 2, join with sl st in top of tch, turn.

Next 8 Rnds: Rep Rnds 6-9, then Rnds 4-7

M, L Only

Rnds 29–34 (35-40): Rep Rnds 8-9 then 4-7.

L Only

Rnds 41–46: Rep last 6 rnds (Rnds 8-9; then Rnds 4-7).

All Sizes

Remove marker.

Fasten off.

FINISHING

Weave in ends. Steam block to schematic measurements.

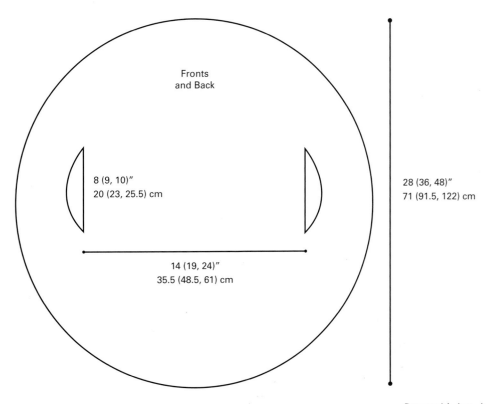

Fronts and Back

8 (9, 10)"
20 (23, 25.5) cm

28 (36, 48)"
71 (91.5, 122) cm

14 (19, 24)"
35.5 (48.5, 61) cm

Lizzy's Lace Mantelet Stitch Pattern Chart

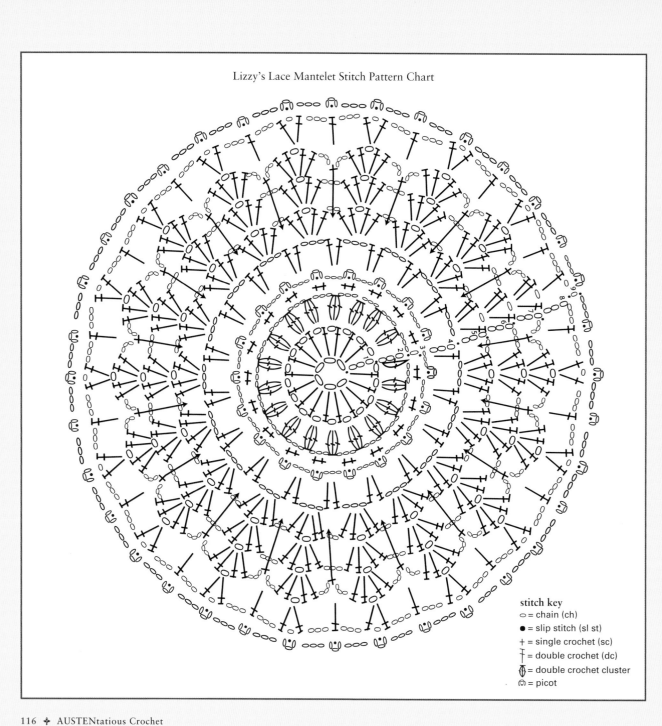

stitch key
○ = chain (ch)
● = slip stitch (sl st)
+ = single crochet (sc)
T = double crochet (dc)
⑂ = double crochet cluster
∞ = picot

SKILL LEVEL

MATERIALS

Patons *Classic Wool* (100% wool;
223 yds/205 m; worsted weight #4
medium): #00224 grey mix (MC)
3 skeins; #00225 dark grey mix (CC1)
2 skeins; #77115 new denim (CC2)
2 skeins

J-10 (6 mm) hk or size needed to
obtain correct gauge

Stitcher's Kit (see page 187)

GAUGE

10 hdc and 7 rows = 4" (10 cm) before
felting

FINISHED SIZES

8" x 62" (20 cm x 1.7 m) after felting

STITCH GUIDE

View an online video demonstrating
how to create this stitch pattern
at: www.stitchscene.com/tutorials

*I*t was only a few years after Jane's passing when crochet became popularized by Queen Victoria. Channel your inner queen and become the quintessence of grace with this fashion-forward design. Worked in one basic stitch and then felted, the result is an exquisite design that is as warm for the wearer as it is beautiful. It can be worn as a traditional scarf might be worn or as a Regency-inspired ruffled collar (as shown in photos). Experiment with a trifecta of colors for a blooming design.

SCARF

Notes: Pm to note beg of each rnd being sure to move marker up with each new rnd. When working inc in marked st replace marker in 2nd st worked. Ch 1 and/or sl st(s) at beg of rows do not count as st(s) throughout. With MC, ch 167.

Rnd 1: Hdc in 2nd ch from hk, hdc in each ch across ending 3 hdc in last ch—168 sts made, rotate work and hdc in each ch across ending 2 hdc in same ch as first hdc, join with sl st in first hdc. *334 sts*

Rnd 2: Ch 1 (do not count as st), 2 hdc in first st, pm, hdc in each st across to 3-hdc group, 2 hdc in each st of this group, pm in 2nd st

of each inc, hdc in each st around to 2-hdc group, 2 hdc in each st of this group, pm in 2nd st of each inc, join with sl st in first ch. *340 sts*

Rnd 3: Ch 1, hdc in each st around working 2 hdc in each marked st, join with sl st in first ch. *346 sts*

Rnd 4: Ch 1, 2 hdc in each st around (move each marker up to same st in current row, as encountered), join with sl st in first ch. *692 sts*

Rnd 5: Rep round 3. *698 sts*

Rnds 6–8: With CC1; rep round 3. *716 sts*

Rnds 9–10: With CC2; rep round 3. *728 sts*

Rnd 11: Ch 1, hdc around working 2 hdc in each marked st, join with sl st in first ch. *734 sts*

Remove markers.

Fasten off.

FINISHING

Weave in ends.

FELTING

Felt (see page 197) until stitches are indiscernible. Wet block by folding scarf in half lengthwise securing only unruffled edge with pins. Shape ruffled edge as desired. When completely dry neatly finish felted scarf (see page 197).

"I wish I could help you in your needlework. I have two hands and a new thimble that lead a very easy life."

—Jane Austen, 1808

SKILL LEVEL

MATERIALS

Rowan Classic *Siena* (100% mercerised cotton; 153 yds/140 m; fingering weight #1 superfine): #659 oak, 10 (12, 13) balls will make all 3 squares

19 (21, 24) La Mode #24793 shank buttons, ⅜" (10 mm), per edge of each square (buttons required for at least 2 edges per square)

F-5 (3.75 mm) hk or size needed to obtain correct gauge

Stitcher's Kit (see page 187)

GAUGE

24 sts (4 wheat sheaves) and 13 rows in Wheat Sheaf Stitch Pattern = 6" (15 cm) blocked.

FINISHED SIZES

XS–L (1X–2X, 3X–4X) has three squares, each 22 (25, 28)"/56 (63.5, 71) cm including edging; assembled rectangular wrap is 22 x 66 (25 x 75, 28 x 84)"/56 x 167.5 (63.5 x 190.5, 71 x 213) cm (squares joined end-to-end); triangular wrap has back length of 31 (35¼, 39½)"/79 (89.5, 100.5) cm (edges of squares joined at points)

STITCH GUIDE

View an online video demonstrating how to create this stitch pattern at: www.stitchscene.com/tutorials

This wrap, designed with Elinor's character in mind, will become an enduring favorite you pull out of your closet again and again. In essence, the design is a combination of three squares joined together by dozens of petite buttons. The key element of this design is its versatility: the squares can be joined in a triangular shape to form a shawl with exquisite drape or all three squares can be buttoned together in a row to create a rectangular wrap. Join just two squares together, leaving center buttons undone for the neckline, and you can have a tunic with a modern edge. Wear over leggings, cinch with a belt—the possibilities and the amusement are endless.

WHEAT SHEAF STITCH PATTERN

Foundation ch is multiple of 5 + 2.

Row 1: Sc in 2nd ch from hk, sc in next ch, *ch 3, skip 2 ch, sc in each of next 3 ch; rep from * across omitting sc at end of last rep, turn.

Row 2: Ch 1 (do not count as st), sc in first sc, *5 dc in ch-3 arch— 1 sheaf made, skip next sc, sc in next sc; rep from * across, turn.

Row 3: Ch 3 (count as hdc and ch 1), skip first 2 sts, sc in each of next 3 dc, *ch 3, skip next 3 sts, sc in each of next 3 dc; rep from * across to last 2 sts, ch 1, hdc in last sc, turn.

Row 4: Ch 3 (count as dc), 2 dc in first ch, skip next sc, sc in next sc, *5 dc in ch-3 arch, skip next sc, sc in next sc; rep from * across to tch, 2 dc in 2nd ch of tch, turn.

Row 5: Ch 1, sc in each of first 2 dc, *ch 3, skip 3 sts, sc in each of next 3 dc; rep from * across omitting 1 sc at end of last rep and working last sc in top of tch, turn.

Rep Rows 2–5 for st patt.

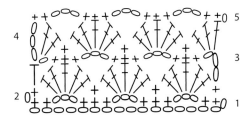

Wheatsheaf Stitch Pattern Chart

stitch key
○ = chain (ch)
+ = single crochet (sc)
Ⲧ = half double crochet (hdc)
Ⲧ = double crochet (dc)

SQUARE

Make 3

Ch 72 (82, 92).

Row 1: Sc in 2nd ch from hk, sc in next ch, *ch 3, skip 2 ch, sc in each of next 3 ch; rep from * across omitting sc at end of last rep, turn. *14 (16, 18) ch-3 arches*

Row 2: Ch 1 (do not count as st), sc in first sc, *5 dc in ch-3 arch, skip next sc, sc in next sc; rep from * across, turn. *14 (16, 18) 5-dc groups*

Row 3: Ch 3 (count as hdc and ch 1)—partial arch made, skip first 2 sts, sc in each of next 3 dc, *ch 3, skip next 3 sts, sc in each of next 3 dc; rep from * to last 2 sts, ch 1, hdc in last sc, turn. *12 (14, 16) ch-3 arches (partial arches not counted throughout)*

Row 4: Ch 3 (count as dc), 2 dc in first ch, skip next sc, sc in next sc, *5 dc in ch-3 arch, skip next sc, sc in next sc; rep from * across to tch, 2 dc in 2nd ch of tch, turn. *12 (14, 16) 5-dc groups*

Row 5: Ch 1 (do not count as st), sc in each of first 2 dc, *ch 3, skip 3 sts, sc in each of next 3 dc; rep from * across omitting 1 sc at end of last rep and working last sc in top of tch, turn. *14 (16, 18) ch-3 arches*

Rep Rows 2–5 until 18½ (21½, 24½)"/47 (54.5, 62) cm from beg ending on Row 3 or 5. Do not turn.

EDGING

Notes: Pm to note beg of rnd being sure to move marker up with each new rnd. Button loop row worked around all edges

Buttonholes and button-loop closures are authentic to the Regency period; zippers are not.

~~~~

so squares can be assembled in any manner and all edges of all squares have same edging.

Rotate work and cont along edge of rows as foll:

Rnd 1: Ch 1 (do not count as st) *3 sc in corner, pm in 2nd sc, 72 (80, 92) sc across edge to next corner; rep from * around, join with sl st in first sc, turn. *300 (332, 380) sts and 5 markers*

Rnd 2: Ch 1 (do not count as st), sc in each sc to first marker—74 (82, 94) sc made, *3 sc in next sc, pm in 2nd sc, sc in each sc to next marker; rep from * around, join with sl st in first sc, turn. *308 (340, 388) sts*

Rnd 3 (button loop rnd): *Sl st in each sc to marker, **3 sl st in next sc—corner worked, remove marker, sl st in next 3 sc, ch 2, remove lp from hk, working left to right skip 2 sl sts just worked, insert hk front to back through next sl st to right, insert hk into dropped lp of ch-2, yo and draw through both lps on hk, 2 sc in same ch-2 lp working right to left, sl st in next unworked sc—button loop made; rep from ** to next marker; rep from * until all 4 sides worked, join with sl st in first sc. *19 (21, 24) button loops on each edge*
Fasten off.

FINISHING

Weave in ends. Steam block to schematic measurements with button loop edges neatly pinned. Sew buttons along center of edging using button loops as placement guides. One edge on at least two squares must have buttons along length to wear finished piece as triangular or rectangular wrap. Buttons need not be placed on all edges, unless desired. More edges with buttons allow for more ways to assemble. To assemble shawl, lay one square with button edging on right vertical edge, place square with no buttons to the right of first square, position third square to right of second with buttons on left edge. Button tog. For triangular wrap, lay square without buttons at diagonal. Position buttoned edgings of two other squares on left and right upper sides of diagonal. Button tog.

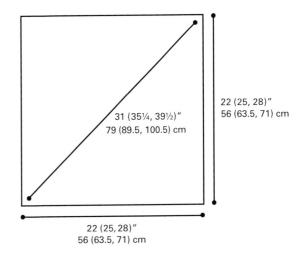

31 (35¼, 39½)"
79 (89.5, 100.5) cm

22 (25, 28)"
56 (63.5, 71) cm

22 (25, 28)"
56 (63.5, 71) cm

All Buttoned Up Assembly Diagram

Edges with buttons

Triangular Wrap

Rectangular Wrap

SKILL LEVEL

MATERIALS

Plymouth *Alpaca Boucle* (90% alpaca, 10% nylon; 65 yds/59 m; bulky weight #5 bulky): 1 skein each of #987 (MC) and #2028 (CC1)

K-10.5 (6.5 mm) hk or size needed to obtain correct gauge

H-8 (5 mm) hk

Stitcher's Kit (see page 187)

GAUGE

11 hdc sts = 4" (10 cm)

FINISHED SIZES

One size fits most: 16" x 3¼" (40.5 x 8 cm) unbuttoned

STITCH GUIDE

View an online video demonstrating how to create this stitch pattern at: www.stitchscene.com/tutorials

---

Borrowed from the boys, the element of fashion characterizing men's attire during the Regency period is no longer just for him. This pattern adds a feminine twist on the popular cravat design, making it just the right neck cloth for her. Stitched in a soft alpaca for comfort with a bit of nylon for stretch, this neck scarf features a simple button closure that creates the flower motif's center. Much more simple to secure than the fussiness of a scarf, just grab and go to add a bit of vintage-styled flirt and English design to your outfit.

LONG SINGLE CROCHET (long sc)

Insert hk in designated st, draw through long lp, keeping lp taut but not tight yo and draw through both lps on hk.

CRAVAT

With MC, ch 32.

SIDE ONE

With larger hk work as foll:

Row 1: Sl st in 2nd ch from hk, sl st in next 6 ch, sc in next 5 ch, hdc in next 7 ch, sc in next 5 ch, sl st in next 7 ch, turn. *31 sts*

Row 2: Ch 1, skip first sl st, sl st in next 6 sts, sc in next 5 sc, hdc in next 7 hdc, sc in next 5 sts, sl st in next 6 sl sts, skip last st. turn. *29 sts*

Row 3: Ch 1, skip first sl st, sl st in next 5 sts, sc in next 5 sc, hdc in next 7 hdc, sc in next 5 sts, sl st in next 5 sl sts, skip last st. *27 sts*

Fasten off.

SIDE TWO

Rotate work so foundation ch is at top. With larger hk and RS facing join yarn to first foundation ch at upper right.

Row 1: Sl st in first 7 ch, sc in next 5 ch, hdc in next 7 ch, sc in next 5 ch, sl st in next 7 ch, turn. *31 sts*

Rows 2–3: Rep Rows 2 and 3 of Side One. Do not fasten off.

BUTTON

With smaller hk, ch 7, join with sl st in 3rd ch, from hk.

Rnd 1: Ch 1, 6 sc in ring join with sl st to first ch.

Rnd 2: Ch 1, 12 long sc through center of ring and around Rnd 1 (see page 126), join with sl st in first ch pull yarn tail through center of ring, to WS.

Rnd 3: Ch 1, sl st in every other st, join with sl st in first ch. *6 sts.* Fasten off leaving 12" (30.5 cm) tail. With tail and tapestry needle whip st (see page 199) in flo of each Rnd 4 st. Pull yarn tightly toward button's center on WS. Knot yarn tails tog.

FLOWER

With CC1 and smaller hk, ch 12, join with sl st in first ch.

Rnd 1: Ch 1, 10 sc in ring, join with sl st in first sc.

Note: Before proceeding, make sure button slips through Rnd 1 ring. If it does not fit, rip out work and make new ring: with more chs if too tight; fewer chs if too loose. (No matter number of chs worked to form ring, Rnd 1 rem same).

Rnd 2: Ch 3 (count as sc and ch-lp), skip next sc, *sc in next st, ch 2, skip next st; rep from * around, join with sc in sl st of Rnd 1. *5 ch-lps*

Rnd 3 (petals): (Sl st, ch 2, 4 dc, ch 2, sl st) in each ch-lp around. *5 petals*

Do not fasten off. Cont by working behind Rnd 3 petals (in Rnd 2) as foll:

Rnd 4: Ch 1, *sc blo (see page 194) of next skipped sc of Rnd 2, ch 4: rep from * around, join with sl st in first sc blo. *5 ch-lps*

Rnd 5 (petals): (Sl st, ch 2, 7 dc, ch 2, sl st) in each ch-lp around. *5 petals.* Fasten off leaving 8" (20 cm) tail.

FINISHING

With tail, sew two outermost petals of flower to end of cravat without button, ensuring flower center remains open for button to be inserted through to close cravat. Weave in ends.

COMMON REGENCY COLORS

Amaranthus: pinkish purple

Aurora: chili colored

Bishop's Blue: purplish blue

Capucine: dark orange

Carmine: rich crimson

Coquelicot: poppy red

Esterhazy: silvery grey

Jonquil: daffodil yellow

Nakara: pearl

Pomona Green: apple green

Primrose: pale yellow

Puce: brownish purple; purplish pink

Spanish blue: dark blue

Vermilion: bright red

CHAPTER 5

Half the Night: Fashions inspired by moonlight

"All was acknowledged,

and half the night

spent in conversation."

—*Pride and Prejudice*

*I*t was not six breaths after Mr. Darcy and Mr. Bingley had left the parlor before Catherine rushed over to Miss Bennet and asked, "So did he propose to you, Jane?" Jane's cheeks colored. She was aware that all eyes had been acutely focused upon her and Mr. Bingley as they had been speaking together this past half hour, but not of proposals. She shook her head no but smiled softly nonetheless.

"Well proposal or not, Jane, anyone can see he is most enamored by you. If only Mr. Tilney felt the same," Catherine sighed heavily. "Toward me, that is. Not toward you," she added. "Not that you don't merit-"

"Well don't count on it," Marianne interrupted. "Either of you. Men are not to be trusted not at all. All charm and no sincerity. And do not, and I mean under no circumstances, let them have a lock of your hair, for one feels quite raped once parted from a curl," she said while brusquely fingering her own tresses.

"Marianne! That's quite enough!" Elinor chastised, her voice firm yet quiet, for one male remained in attendance. She glanced at Edmund, still conversing with Fanny in a nearby corner of the room.

Elinor directed the three heroines toward the rest of us who had just taken up our stitching around the newly lit fire. As the sun left, a chill arrived; the crisp autumn nights would now require a shawl. I saw Fanny reach for hers as Edmund asked if anyone would care to join Fanny and him out in the garden to star gaze.

"I shall," announced Marianne as she rose from her seat, only to be pulled back down by Elinor on her right and Emma on her left.

"Remember your cold," spoke Elinor pointedly.

"My cold?"

"Yes your cold," reminded Emma, motioning for Fanny and Edmund to go on while at the same time adeptly pinning Marianne between her and Elinor.

After the couple had disappeared on the terrace, Elinor said, "For someone who is all too often filled with sensibilities, you are entirely without any at this present time."

"What?" exclaimed Marianne. "Fanny and Edmund? Surely not. She shows no emotion whatsoever. If there be love, one must show it or howsoever should a gentleman know?"

"And that has worked so well for you," said Elizabeth. She returned her focus to Jane. "It appeared Mr. Bingley might take you out the terrace at any moment to propose, his mannerisms unsettled as they were. If he did not propose, what did he speak of that made him appear so anxious?"

"Rabbits," Jane said. "He spoke of rabbits."

"Rabbits?" they all inquired.

"Yes, rabbits. I had pointed to the playful antics of one outside on the lawn and he informed me there was quite an abundance of rabbits at Netherfield," she said. "And quail. He said there was much quail. He invited father to hunt them."

"That's promising," encouraged Elizabeth. Marianne choked. Elizabeth ignored her and continued. "Then what?"

"Fox. Mr. Bingley said there is a prolific amount of fox," said Jane.

Elizabeth laughed. "He is quite besotted, Jane. A proposal is forthcoming, I assure you." Jane smiled.

"Are you joking?" asked Marianne, flummoxed. "Why do you encourage her? Extolling at length about various animals is not a sign of love. Has Mr. Bingley recited poetry to you yet, Jane? Or what of his own verse? Has he written an ode to your beauty?"

Jane's smile dimmed uncertain. "No, he has not."

"But," said Elizabeth, "It is a truth universally acknowledged that if a single man in possession of a good fortune cannot speak intelligibly in the presence of a certain woman, he is sure to want her as a wife."

DREAMING OF
~ MR. KNIGHTLEY PAJAMA SET ~

SKILL LEVEL

MATERIALS

Aunt Lydia's *Bamboo Crochet Thread Size 3* (100% Bamboo; 150 yds/137 m; crochet thread): #305 wheat (MC) 5 (6, 7, 8, 9) balls for corset and 9 (10 11, 12, 13) balls for knickers; #12 black (CC1) 1 skein for corset

E-4 (3.5 mm) hk or size needed to obtain correct gauge

¾" (19 mm) wide elastic matching length to body waist circumference + 1" (2.5 cm)

¼" (6 mm) black satin ribbon, 84" (213) cm long

Stitcher's Kit (see page 187)

GAUGE

20 sc and 24 Rows = 4" (10 cm)

FINISHED SIZES

XS (S, M, L, 1X) has bust of 32½ (35, 37, 41½, 45¾)"/82.5 (89, 94, 105.5, 116) cm and hip circumference of 36½ (39½, 42, 45¼, 49¼)"/93 (100.5, 107, 114.5, 125) cm

Note: Knicker waist must be large enough to pull over hips. Elastic will gather excess fabric for custom fit at waist.

STITCH GUIDE

View an online video demonstrating how to create this stitch pattern at: www.stitchscene.com/tutorials

This stylish corset and knickers-inspired design calls to mind lofty four-poster beds and crisp white linens. Worked in a fine bamboo thread, this pajama set is a modern twist on Regency undergarments. The sassy knickers feature an easy and comfortable elasticized waist as well as playful ruffles with black ribbon accent. Corded stitching worked along the hem, arms, and neckline creates a finished corset edge. Be the vintage vixen while you curl up with a steaming cup of cocoa, a good book, and your Mr. Knightley.

SINGLE CROCHET DECREASE (sc2tog)

Insert hk in st, draw through lp, insert hk in next st, draw through lp, yo and draw through all 3 lps on hk.

REVERSE SINGLE CROCHET STITCH (rev sc)

Working from left to right, insert hk in st to right, work sc (yo and draw through st, yo and draw through 2 lps on hk).

Note: Ch 1 and/or sl st(s) at beg of rows do not count as st(s) throughout.

CORSET FRONT

Make 2

Worked from shoulder to hem.

With MC, ch 11 (12, 13, 13, 15).

Row 1: Sc in 2nd ch from hk and in each ch across, turn. *10 (11, 12, 12, 14) sts*

FIRST SHOULDER SHAPING

Row 2: Ch 1, 2 sc in first st—inc made at neckline, sc across, turn. *11 (12, 13, 13, 15) sts*

Rows 3–4: Ch 1, sc in each st, turn.

Row 5: Ch 1, sc across ending 2 sc in last st, turn. *12 (13, 14, 14, 16) sts*

Next 18 Rows: Work in sc working inc row (Row 5) every 2nd row for 9 times. *21 (22, 23, 23, 25) sts*

Row 24: 2 sc in each of first 2 sts—inc made at neckline, sc across, turn. *23 (24, 25, 25, 27) sts*

Next 4 Rows: Work in sc AT SAME TIME inc neckline as foll: 2 (2, 2, 2, 1) sts for 1 row, 1 st for 1 row, 2 (2, 1, 1, 1) sts for 1 row, then 1 st for 1 row. *29 (30, 30, 30, 31) sts*

Next 4 Rows: Work in sc AT SAME TIME inc neckline as foll: 2 sts for 1 row, 1 st for 1 row, 0 (1, 1, 2, 2) st for 1 row, then 0 (0, 0, 1, 1) st for 1 row. *32 (34, 34, 36, 37) sts*

L, 1X Only

Next 2 Rows: Ch 1, sc across, turn.

All Sizes: Cont with Armhole Shaping.

ARMHOLE SHAPING

Row 33 (33, 33, 35, 35) (inc row): Ch 1, 2 sc in first st—inc made at side armhole, sc across, turn. *33 (35, 35, 37, 38) sts*

Next 2 Rows: Ch 1, sc across, turn.

Next Row: Ch 1, sc across ending 2 sc in last st, turn. *34 (36, 36, 38, 39) sts*

Next 2 Rows: Ch 1, sc across, turn.

Next 3 (5, 6, 8, 11) Rows: Work in sc AT SAME TIME inc 1 st at armhole every row for 3 (5, 6, 5, 5) times, then 0 (0, 0, 3, 6) sts every row for 0 (0, 0, 3, 6) times. *37 (41, 42, 49, 56) sts*

Next 7 (5, 10, 6, 9) Rows: Ch 1, sc across, turn.

SIDE SEAM AND WAIST SHAPING

Row 49 (49, 55, 55, 61) (dec row): Ch 1, sc2tog (see page 132)—dec at seam side made, sc across, turn. *36 (40, 41, 48, 55) sts*

Next 36 (42, 36, 42, 36) Rows: Work in sc AT SAME TIME dec 1 st at side seam every 6th row for 6 (7, 6, 7, 6) times, *30 (33, 35, 41, 49) sts*

Next 3 (1, 4, 3, 5) Rows: Ch 1, sc across, turn.

HIP SHAPING

Row 89 (93, 96, 101, 103) (inc row): Ch 1, 2 sc in first st—inc made at side seam, sc across, turn. *31 (34, 36, 42, 50) sts*

Next 1 (2, 1, 2, 1) Rows: Work in sc AT SAME TIME inc 1 st at side seam every row. *32 (36, 37, 44, 51) sts*

Next 19 (16, 17, 17, 18) Rows: Work in sc AT SAME TIME inc 1 st at side seam every 4th row for 4 (1, 2, 2, 3) times, then every 3rd row for 1 (4, 3, 3, 2) time. *37 (41, 42, 49, 56) sts*

Next 0 (0, 1, 1, 1) Row: Ch 1, sc across, turn.

HEM SHAPING

Row 110 (112, 116, 122, 124): Ch 1, sc across leaving last 3 sts unworked—dec made at side seam, turn. *34 (38, 39, 46, 53) sts*

Next Row: Sl st in first 5 sts—dec made at side seam, sc across, turn. *29 (33, 33, 41, 48) sts*

Next 7 (8, 8, 7, 9) Rows: Work in sc AT SAME TIME dec at side seam 3 (3, 3, 5, 6) sts for 4 (5, 2, 7, 7) rows and 4 (4, 4, 0, 0) sts for 3 (2, 4, 0, 0) rows. Work even for 0 (1, 2, 0, 2) rows. *5 (5, 5, 6, 6) sts*

L Only

Next Row: Ch 1, sc across.

Fasten off.

CORSET RIGHT FRONT BAND

With WS facing, join MC center front of Right Front at neckline edge.

Row 1: Ch 1, work 74 (74, 79, 79, 83) evenly spaced sc along front edge, turn.

Row 2: Ch 1, sc blo in each st across, turn.

Rows 3–7: Ch 1, sc across, turn.

Fasten off.

LACING LOOPS

With RS facing, join CC1 to flo of first st of Left Front Band Row 2.

Row 1: Sc flo in each Row 2 st to top of band (neckline edge), turn. *74 (74, 79, 79, 83) sts*

XS, S, 1X Only

Row 2: Ch 1, sc in first 2 sts, *ch 3, skip 3 sc, sc in next 4 sts; rep from * 8 (8, 9) times, ch 3, skip 3 sc, sc in next 2 (2, 4) sts, ch 2, skip 2 sc, sc in last 2 sts. *11 (11, 12) ch-lps*

M, L Only

Row 2: Ch 1, sc in first 2 sts, *ch 3, skip 3 sc, 4 sc; rep from * 9 times, (ch 2, skip 2 sc, sc in next 2 sts) twice. *11 ch-lps*

Fasten off.

CORSET LEFT FRONT BAND

With RS facing, join MC to hem edge of center front of Left Front. Rep Right Front Band.

CORSET BACK

Worked from hem to shoulder.

Ch 75 (81, 87, 97, 107).

Row 1: Sc in 2nd ch from hk and each ch across, turn. *74 (80, 86, 96, 106) sts*

Rows 2–5: Ch 1, sc across, turn.

Row 6: Ch 1, sc2tog, sc across to last 2 sts, sc2tog, turn. *72 (78, 84, 94, 104) sts*

Next 12 (12, 12, 12, 14) Rows: Work in sc AT SAME TIME dec 1 st at each edge every 3rd row for 4 times, then every 2nd row for 0 (0, 0, 0, 1) time. *64 (70, 76, 86, 94) sts*

Next 4 (4, 4, 4, 8) Rows: Ch 1, sc across, turn.

Row 23 (23, 23, 23, 29): Ch 1, 2 sc in first st, sc across ending 2 sc in last st. *66 (72, 78, 88, 96) sts*

Next 35 (35, 40, 40, 34) Rows: Work in sc AT SAME TIME inc 1 st at each edge every 6th row for 1 (1, 1, 1, 0) times, every 4th row once, then every 5th row for 5 (5, 6, 6, 6) times. *80 (86, 94, 104, 110) sts*

Next 10 (10, 8, 10, 9) Rows: Ch 1, sc across, turn.

ARMHOLE SHAPING

Row 69 (69, 72, 74, 73): Sl st in first 1 (1, 2, 2, 2) st, sc across leaving last 1 (1, 2, 2, 2) st unworked, turn. *78 (84, 90, 100, 106) sts*

Next Row: Sl st in first 1 (1, 1, 2, 2) st, sc across leaving last 1 (1, 1, 2, 2) st unworked, turn. *76 (82, 88, 96, 102) sts*

Next 2 Rows: Sl st in first 1 (1, 1, 1, 2) st, sc across leaving last 1 (1, 1, 1, 2) st unworked, turn. *72 (78, 84, 92, 94) sts*

Next 3 (3, 2, 2, 2) Rows: Ch 1, sc across, turn.

Row 76 (76, 78, 80, 79) (dec row): Sl st in first st, sc across leaving last st unworked, turn. *70 (76, 82, 90, 92) sts*

Next 2 Rows: Rep last 2 rows (work even for 1 row, then work dec row once). *68 (74, 80, 88, 90) sts*

L, XL Only

Next (15, 6) Rows: Work in sc AT SAME TIME dec 1 st each edge every 6th row for (1, 0) time, then every 3rd row for (3, 2) times. *(82, 86) sts*

Next 21 (23, 25, 12, 26) Rows: Ch 1, sc across, turn.

FIRST SHOULDER SHAPING

Row 100 (102, 106, 110, 114) (short row): Ch 1, sc in first 31 (32, 34, 36, 37) sts, turn.

Next Row: Sl st in first 5 sts—dec made at neckline, sc across, turn. *26 (27, 29, 31, 32) sts*

Next Row (short row): Ch 1, sc in next 22 (23, 25, 24, 26) sts, turn.

Next Row: Sl st in first 3 sts, sc across, turn. *19 (20, 22, 21, 23) sts*

Next 6 Rows: Work in sc AT SAME time dec 2 sts at neckline edge for next 2 rows; 1 st for 1 row; 2 sts for 1 row; then 1 st for 2 rows. *10 (11, 12, 12, 14) sts* Fasten off.

OPPOSITE SHOULDER SHAPING

Join MC at opposite edge of last full row [Row 99, 99, 105, 109, 113). Rep First Shoulder Shaping.

CORSET FINISHING

Sew shoulder and side seams. Work 1 row evenly spaced rev sc (see page 132) around neckline, hemline and armholes. Weave in ends. Steam block to schematic measurements, pinning front lace loops to lay flat. Thread ribbon through loops.

KNICKERS FRONT

Note: Ch 1 and/or sl st(s) at beg of rows do not count as st(s) throughout.

Make 2

With MC, ch 36 (39, 41, 44, 47).

Row 1: Sc in 2nd ch from hk and in each ch across, turn. *35 (38, 40, 43, 46) sts*

Rows 2–4: Ch 1, sc across, turn.

Row 5: Ch 1, sc across ending 2 sc in last st—inc made at inseam, turn. *36 (39, 41, 44, 47) sts*

Rows 6–8: Ch 1, sc across, turn.

Row 9: Ch 1, 2 sc in first st, sc across ending 2 sc in last st— inc made at both inseam and side seam, turn. *38 (41, 43, 46, 49) sts*

XS, S, M, L Only

Next 8 Rows: Work in sc AT SAME TIME inc 1 st at inseam every 4th (2nd, 2nd, 2nd) row for 2 times, then every 4th row for 0 (1, 1, 1) time. *40 (44, 46, 49) sts*

1X Only

Next 8 Rows: Work in sc AT SAME TIME inc 1 st at inseam

every 2nd row once, 1 st at both edges every 2nd row once, then 1 st at inseam every 2nd row twice. *54 sts*

All Sizes

Next Row: Ch 1, sc across, turn.

Row 19: Ch 1, 2 sc in first sc—inc made at side seam, sc across, turn. *41 (45, 47, 50, 55) sts*

Next 6 (4, 4, 4, 4) Rows: Work in sc AT SAME TIME, inc 1 st at inseam every 2nd row for 1 (1, 2, 2, 2) times, then every 4th row for 1 (0, 0, 0, 0) time; work even for 0 (2, 0, 0, 0) row. *43 (46, 49, 52, 57) sts.*

Next 3 (3, 1, 1, 1) Rows: Ch 1, sc across, turn.

Next Row: Ch 1, 2 sc in first st, sc across ending 2 sc in last st, turn. *45 (48, 51, 54, 59) sts*

XS, S, M Only

Next 4 (2, 2) Rows: Ch 1, sc across, turn.

All Sizes

Next 2 (6, 6, 8, 8) Rows: Work in sc AT SAME TIME inc 1 st at inseam every 2nd row for 0 (0, 0, 1, 1) times; inc 1 st at both inseam and side seam every 2nd row for 0 (1, 1, 1, 1) time; then inc 1 st at inseam every 2nd (4th, 4th, 4th, 4th) row once; work even for 0 (1, 1, 3, 1) row. *46 (51, 54, 58, 63) sts*

Next 4 (6, 8, 8, 8) Rows: Work in sc AT SAME TIME inc 1 st at both inseam and side seam every 2nd (4th, 4th, 4th, 4th) row once; inc 1 st at inseam every 2nd row once; then inc 1 st at side seam every 2nd row for 0 (0, 1, 1, 1) time. *49 (54, 58, 62, 67) sts*

XS Only

Next 2 Rows: Ch 1, sc across, turn.

All Sizes

Next 4 Rows: Work in sc AT SAME TIME inc 1 st at inseam

every 2nd row and inc 1 st at both inseam and side seam every 2nd row once. *51 (57, 61, 65, 70) sts*

Rows (46-51, 46-50, 46-48, 46, 46): Ch 1, sc across, turn.

XS Only

Row 52: Ch 1, 2 sc in first sc, sc across, turn. *53 sts*

All Sizes

Next 2 Rows: Ch 1, sc across, turn.

All Sizes

Cont with Hip and Crotch shaping.

HIP AND CROTCH SHAPING

Row 55 (53, 51, 49, 49): Ch 1, sc across leaving last 2 (2, 3, 3, 3) sts unworked—dec made at crotch, turn. *51 (55, 58, 62, 67) sts*

Next Row: Sl st in first 2 sts, sc across, turn. *49 (53, 56, 60, 65) sts*

Next Row: Ch 1, 2 sc in first 0 (1, 1, 1, 1) st—inc made at hip (except XS), sc across leaving last 2 sts unworked—dec made at crotch. *47 (52, 55, 59, 64) sts*

Next 5 (7, 7, 7, 7) Rows: Work in sc AT SAME TIME dec 1 (1, 1, 2, 2) st at crotch for first row; then dec 1 st at crotch every 2nd row for 2 (3, 3, 3, 3) times. *44 (48, 51, 54, 59) sts*

XS Only

Next 2 Rows: Ch 1, sc across, turn.

All Sizes

Row 65 (63, 61, 59, 59): Ch 1, 2 sc in first st—inc made at hip, sc across, turn. *45 (49, 52, 55, 60) sts*

XS, S, M, L Only

Next 3 Rows: Ch 1, sc across, turn.

1X Only

Next 3 Rows: Work in sc AT SAME TIME dec 1 st at crotch in 1st row; then inc 1 st at hip in 3rd row. *60 sts*

All Sizes

Next 3 Rows: Ch 1, sc across, turn.

Next Row: Ch 1, 2 sc in first st, sc across, turn. *46 (50, 53, 56, 61) sts*

Next 20 Rows: Ch 1, sc across, turn.

Row 93 (91, 89, 87, 87): Ch 1, sc2tog—dec made at hip, sc across, turn. *45 (49, 52, 55, 60) sts*

Next 14 (14, 14, 12, 12) Rows: Work in sc AT SAME TIME dec 1 st at hip every 6th row twice, then every 2nd row for 1 (1, 1, 0, 0) time. *42 (46, 49, 53, 58) sts*

Next 2 (3, 3, 5, 5) Rows: Ch 1, sc across, turn.

S, M, L, 1X Only

Row (109, 107, 105, 105): Ch 1, sc2tog—dec made at hip, sc across, turn. *45 (48, 52, 57) sts*

M, L, 1X Only

Next 2 Rows: Work in sc AT SAME TIME dec 1 st at hip every 2nd row. *47 (51, 56) sts*

L and 1X Only

Rows 108-109: Ch 1, sc across, turn.

All Sizes

Fasten off. Temporarily label as Front.

KNICKERS BACK

Make 2

With MC, ch 47 (51, 53, 57, 61).

Work as for Front to Hip and Crotch Shaping. *64 (69, 73, 78, 84) sts*

HIP AND CROTCH SHAPING

Row 55 (53, 51, 49, 49): Ch 1, 2 sc in first 0 (0, 0, 1, 1,) st, sc across leaving last 3 (3, 3, 4, 5) sts unworked—dec made at crotch, turn. *61 (66, 70, 75, 80) sts*

Next 4 Rows: Work in sc AT SAME TIME dec 2 (2, 3, 3, 3) sts at inseam once, 2 sts at inseam once, 1 (2, 2, 2, 2) sts at inseam once, then 2 (2, 2, 1, 1) st once. *54 (58, 61, 67, 72) sts*

Next Row: Ch 1, sc across to last 2 sts, sc2tog—dec made at crotch, turn. *53 (57, 60, 66, 71) sts*

Next 6 Rows: Work in sc AT SAME TIME dec 1 st at crotch and inc 1 st at side seam once; dec 1 st at inseam for 5 (4, 4, 4, 4) rows; then dec 1 st at inseam and inc 1 st side seam for 0 (1, 1, 1, 1) time. *48 (53, 56, 62, 67) sts*

Next 4 Rows: Work in sc AT SAME TIME dec 1 st at inseam every 2nd row for 0 (0, 0, 1, 1) time; then dec 1 st at inseam and inc 1 st at inseam every 2nd row once. *48 (53, 56, 61, 66) sts*

Next 7 Rows: Work in sc AT SAME TIME dec 0 (1, 1, 1, 2) sts every 3rd row once; then dec 0 (0, 0, 1, 1) st every 4th row once. *48 (52, 55, 59, 63) sts*

Next 3 (5, 7, 9, 9) Rows: Ch 1, sc across, turn.

Row 81: Ch 1, sc across leaving last st unworked, turn. *47 (51, 54, 58, 62) sts*

Next 9 (7, 5, 3, 3) Rows: Ch 1, sc across, turn.

Row 91 (89, 87, 85, 85): Ch 1, sc2tog, sc across, turn. *46 (50, 53, 57, 61) sts*

Next 1 (1, 5, 5, 5) Row: Ch 1, sc across, turn.

Next Row: Ch 1, sc2tog, sc across leaving last st unworked, turn. *44 (48, 51, 55, 59) sts*

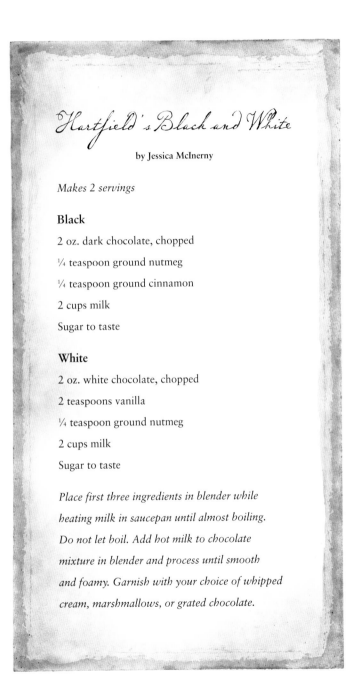

Hartfield's Black and White

by Jessica McInerny

Makes 2 servings

Black

2 oz. dark chocolate, chopped

¼ teaspoon ground nutmeg

¼ teaspoon ground cinnamon

2 cups milk

Sugar to taste

White

2 oz. white chocolate, chopped

2 teaspoons vanilla

¼ teaspoon ground nutmeg

2 cups milk

Sugar to taste

Place first three ingredients in blender while heating milk in saucepan until almost boiling. Do not let boil. Add hot milk to chocolate mixture in blender and process until smooth and foamy. Garnish with your choice of whipped cream, marshmallows, or grated chocolate.

Next 8 (8, 4, 4, 4) Rows: Ch 1, sc across, turn.

Next 6 Rows: Work in sc AT SAME TIME dec 1 st at side seam every 3rd row twice. *42 (46 ,49, 53, 57) sts*

Next 2 (3, 3, 2, 2) Rows: Ch 1, sc across, turn.

S, M, L, 1X Only

Row (109, 107, 104, 104): Ch 1, sc2tog, sc across, turn. *(45, 48, 52, 56) sts*

M, L, 1X Only

Row (108, 105, 105): Ch 1, sc across, turn.

Row (109, 107, 107): Ch 1, sc2tog, sc across, turn. *(47, 51, 55) sts*

L and 1X Only

Rows 108–109: Ch 1, sc across.

Fasten off.

KNICKERS FINISHING

Steam block to schematic measurements. Sew Left Back and Front tog along inner and outer leg. Rep for Right Front and Back. Sew pieces tog along center front, crotch, and center back. Weave in ends. Make elastic casing (see page 198).

KNICKERS RUFFLE

Pm to note beg of each rnd being sure to move marker up with each new rnd.

With RS facing join MC to leg hem at inseam.

Rnd 1: Ch 1, work even number of sc around, join with sl st in first sc, turn.

Rnd 2: Ch 3 (count as hdc and ch 1), *hdc in next st, ch 1; rep from *around, join with sl st in 2nd ch of tch, turn.

Rnd 3: Ch 1, sc in each hdc and ch-sp around, join with sl st in first sc, turn.

Rnd 4: Ch 1, hdc in first sc, *ch 2, hdc in next sc; rep from * around, join with sl st in first hdc, turn.

Rnd 5: Ch 1, hdc in first hdc, *ch 3, hdc in next hdc; rep from * around, join with sl st in first hdc, turn.

Rnd 6: Ch 1, hdc in first hdc, *ch 4, hdc in next hdc; rep from * around, join with sl st in first hdc, turn.

Rnd 7: Ch 1, hdc in first hdc, *ch 5, hdc in next hdc; rep from * around, join with sl st in first hdc.

Fasten off.

KNICKERS RUFFLE FINISHING

Weave in ends. Thread ribbon through Rnd 2 of ruffle and tie bow.

CORSET

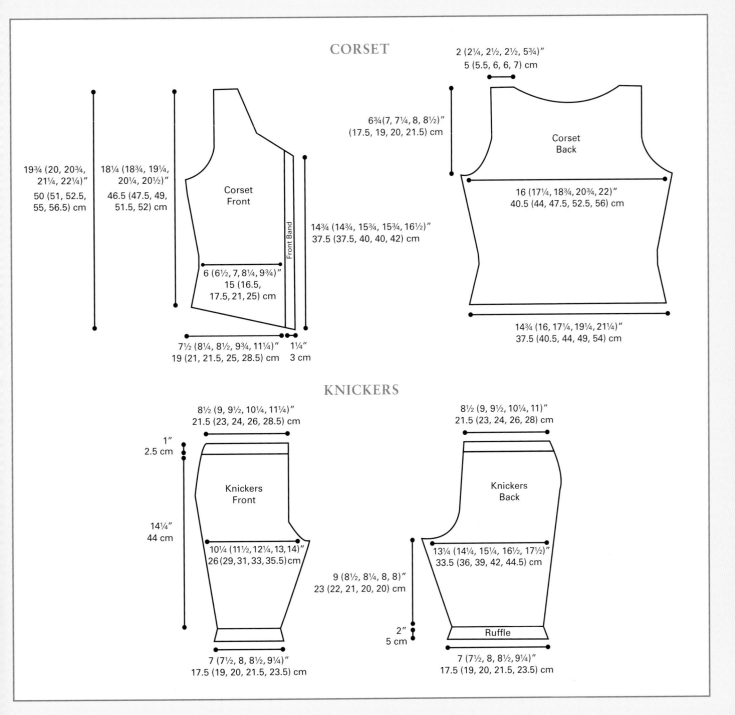

2 (2¼, 2½, 2½, 5¾)"
5 (5.5, 6, 6, 7) cm

6¾(7, 7¼, 8, 8½)"
(17.5, 19, 20, 21.5) cm

Corset
Back

16 (17¼, 18¾, 20¾, 22)"
40.5 (44, 47.5, 52.5, 56) cm

14¾ (16, 17¼, 19¼, 21¼)"
37.5 (40.5, 44, 49, 54) cm

19¾ (20, 20¾, 21¼, 22¼)"
50 (51, 52.5, 55, 56.5) cm

18¼ (18¾, 19¼, 20¼, 20½)"
46.5 (47.5, 49, 51.5, 52) cm

Corset
Front

Front Band

14¾ (14¾, 15¾, 15¾, 16½)"
37.5 (37.5, 40, 40, 42) cm

6 (6½, 7, 8¼, 9¾)"
15 (16.5, 17.5, 21, 25) cm

7½ (8¼, 8½, 9¾, 11¼)"
19 (21, 21.5, 25, 28.5) cm

1¼"
3 cm

KNICKERS

8½ (9, 9½, 10¼, 11¼)"
21.5 (23, 24, 26, 28.5) cm

8½ (9, 9½, 10¼, 11)"
21.5 (23, 24, 26, 28) cm

1"
2.5 cm

Knickers
Front

Knickers
Back

14¼"
44 cm

10¼ (11½, 12¼, 13, 14)"
26 (29, 31, 33, 35.5) cm

13¼ (14¼, 15¼, 16½, 17½)"
33.5 (36, 39, 42, 44.5) cm

9 (8½, 8¼, 8, 8)"
23 (22, 21, 20, 20) cm

2"
5 cm

Ruffle

7 (7½, 8, 8½, 9¼)"
17.5 (19, 20, 21.5, 23.5) cm

7 (7½, 8, 8½, 9¼)"
17.5 (19, 20, 21.5, 23.5) cm

MATERIALS

Fibra Natura *Flax* (100% linen; 137 yds/125 m; dk weight #3 light): #14 white (MC) 1 skein

DMC *Senso Microfiber Cotton* (60% cotton, 40% acrylic; 150 yds/137 m; cotton thread size 3): #1104 pink (CC1) 1 ball

B-1 (2.25 mm) hk or size needed to obtain correct gauge

1⅝ (1¾, 1¾, 2, 2, 2¼) yds/1.5 (1.6, 1.6, 1.8, 1.8, 2) m cotton eyelet fabric, 36" (90 cm) wide with finished border on one lengthwise edge

Stitcher's Kit (see page 187)

GAUGE

20 sc and 16 rows = 4" (10 cm)

FINISHED SIZES

XS (S, M, L, 1X, 2X) has bust circumference of 33 (36, 38, 41, 45, 48½)"/84 (91.5, 96.5, 104, 114, 123) cm. There is ample ease (see page 188) for sleeping comfort.

STITCH GUIDE

View an online video demonstrating how to create this stitch pattern at: www.stitchscene.com/tutorials

One can easily envision Lizzy and Jane whispering through the nights of their engagements wearing this ethereally elegant, but not in the least sugary nightgown. A staple of Regency undergarments, this chemise features a crocheted linen yoke to provide soft and airy bedroom comfort. Don't be intimated by the sewing that accompanies the crochet—the design has only two simple side seams if you choose an eyelet cotton fabric with an already finished hem. In just a few hours you can make yourself a graceful chemise perfect for Regency dreaming.

PICOT STITCH

Ch 3, sl st in 3rd ch from hk.

BACK YOKE

Note: Ch 1 at beg of row does not count as st throughout.

With MC, ch 19.

Row 1: Sc in 2nd ch from hk and in each ch across, turn. *18 sts*

Row 2 (ch-row): Ch 1, sc in first 4 sc, ch 10, skip 10 sts, sc in last 4 sc, turn.

Rep ch-row (Row 2) until yoke is 11¼ (12, 12½, 13, 14, 14¼)"/28.5 (30.5, 32, 33, 35.5, 36) cm from beg.

Note: Total number ch-rows completed must be multiple of 2.

Next Row: Ch 1, sc in each st across.

Fasten off.

In the 2005 *Pride and Prejudice* film with Keira Knightly, Mrs. Bennet and her daughters dye their clothing with beetroot juice. If you desire the subdued colors of the time, and are feeling a bit adventurous, purchase bare wool or cotton for any of the projects and do the same. For the Confessions Chemise, the brightly bleached white eyelet fabric was dipped in tea prior to sewing to match the more natural colored linen fibers of the crocheted yoke.

FRONT YOKE

With MC, ch 15.

Row 1: Sc in 2nd ch from hk and in each ch across, turn.

14 sts

Row 2 (ch-row): Ch 1, sc in first 3 sc, ch 8, skip 8 sts, sc in last 3 sc, turn.

Rep ch-row (Row 2) until yoke is 11¼ (12, 12½, 13, 14, 14¼)" /28.5 (30.5, 32, 33, 35.5, 36) cm from beg.

Note: Total number ch-rows must be multiple of 2.

Next Row: Ch 1, sc in each st across.

Fasten off.

LACING

Work on Back and Front Yokes.

See Lacing Diagram.

With CC1, make foundation chain four times length of yoke—lacing made.

Thread lacing through tapestry needle.

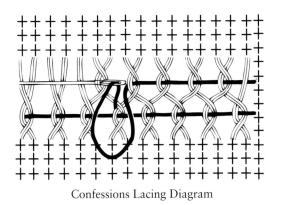

Confessions Lacing Diagram

stitch key
+ = single crochet (sc)

Row 1: Working from right to left press tip of needle against 2nd ch-row pulling it over first ch-row—2 ch-rows crossed. Pull lacing through middle (from back to front) and keep lacing taut to hold ch-rows in position. Cont working over pairs of ch-rows in same manner. At left edge thread lacing through vertical sc row.

Rotate work so opposite side of yoke is closest to you.

Row 2: Thread lacing under first ch-row (skipped to stagger lacing points). Cont lacing as before. Thread lacing through vertical sc row. Rotate work so opposite side of yoke is again closest to you.

Row 3: Rep Row 1.

Row 4: Rep Row 2.

Using yarn tails, secure lacing. Weave in ends.

EDGING

With MC and Back Yoke, work 1 row of evenly spaced (sc, ch 3, sl st in first ch—picot made sc) around and working picot in each corner.

Rep Edging on Front Yoke.

SHOULDER STRAP

Make 2

With MC, ch 4.

Row 1: Sc in 2nd ch from hk and each st across. *3 sts*

Row 2: Ch 1, sc across.

Rep Row 2 until 6 (6½, 7, 7½ ¼, 8, 8¾)"/15 (16.5, 17.5, 18, 20, 22) cm from beg.

Note: Straps fit tightly at this stage as linen lengthens when blocked.

Fasten off.

Wet block yokes and straps to schematic measurements.

FINISHING

Using Front and Back Fabric schematics as guide, cut 1 back
and 1 front of gown from fabric. Place right sides tog and
sew both seam sides ½" (13 mm) from matched edges.
Along top (bust) edge, sew 2 rows of long straight stitches
and draw threads to gather edge to same size as crocheted
yoke. Overlap lower edge of Front Yoke on top of upper edge
of Front Gown. Sew tog. Join Back Yoke to Back Gown in
same manner. Pin straps to inside of yokes. Adjust straps
to fit, and then securely sew in place.

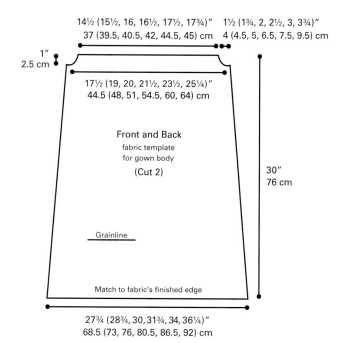

11½ (12½, 12¾, 13¼, 14¼, 14½)"
29 (31, 32.5, 33.5, 36, 37) cm

3¼"
8.5 cm
Front Yoke

11½ (12½, 12¾, 13¼, 14¼, 14½)"
29 (31, 32.5, 33.5, 36, 37) cm

4"
10 cm
Back Yoke

6 (7, 8, 9, 10, 11)"
15 (17.5, 20, 23, 25.5, 28) cm

½"
1.25 cm
Straps

14½ (15½, 16, 16½, 17½, 17¾)"   1½ (1¾, 2, 2½, 3, 3¾)"
37 (39.5, 40.5, 42, 44.5, 45) cm   4 (4.5, 5, 6.5, 7.5, 9.5) cm

1"
2.5 cm

17½ (19, 20, 21½, 23½, 25¼)"
44.5 (48, 51, 54.5, 60, 64) cm

Front and Back
fabric template
for gown body
(Cut 2)

30"
76 cm

Grainline

Match to fabric's finished edge

27¾ (28¾, 30, 31¾, 34, 36¼)"
68.5 (73, 76, 80.5, 86.5, 92) cm

*Which two sisters
married the same day?*

Find out on page 203.

SKILL LEVEL

MATERIALS

Lion Brand *Moonlight Mohair* (57% Acrylic, 28% Mohair, 9% cotton, 6% metallic polyester; 82 yds/66666675 m; chunky weight #5 bulky): #510-205 glacier bay 3 skeins

K-10.5 (6.5 mm) hk or size needed to obtain correct gauge

Stitcher's Kit (see page 187)

Aleene's Tacky Glue

GAUGE

5-point star = 5½" (14 cm) diameter

FINISHED SIZES

25" x 69" (63.5 x 1.8 m)

STITCH GUIDE

View an online video demonstrating how to create this stitch pattern at: www.stitchscene.com/tutorials

nchant admirers in this light and airy mohair stole. Large stars are encircled by smaller five-pointed stars designed to create an ethereal night sky to wear softly about your shoulders. Motifs are each worked separately and then joined together, making this an easy project to carry with you. The option of fitting the shawl to your body by draping it around your shoulders like a wide scarf and then cinching the wrap at your waist with the belt of your choice adds a modern twist.

PICOT STITCH

Ch 3, sl st in 3rd ch from hk.

Note: For all stars, do not turn at end of each rnd. Leave 8" (20 cm) tail on each motif for joining.

SMALL FIVE-POINT STAR

Make 26

Ch 6, join with sl st in first ch.

Rnd 1: Ch 1, 10 sc in ring, join with sl st in ch.

Rnd 2: *Ch 6, sl st in 3rd ch from hk, ch 3, skip 1 sc, sl st in next sc; rep from * around.

Fasten off.

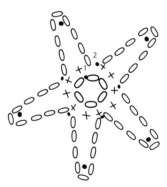

stitch key
○ = chain (ch)
● = slip stitch (sl st)
+ = single crochet (sc)

5 pointed Star Stitch Chart

MEDIUM EIGHT-POINT STAR

Make 2

Ch 6, join with sl st in first ch .

Rnd 1: Ch 1, 16 sc in ring, join with sl st in ch 1.

Rnd 2: *Ch 7, sl st in 3rd ch from hk—picot made, ch 4, skip 1 sc, sl st in next sc, ch 6, sl st in 3rd ch from hk, ch 3, skip sc, sl st in next sc, ch 5, sl st in 3rd ch from hk, ch 2, skip 1 sc, sl st in next sc, ch 6, sl st in 3rd ch from hk, ch 3, skip sc, sl st in next sc; rep from * around.

Fasten off.

"Go, by all means, my dear; only put on a white gown; Miss Tilney always wears white."

—Northanger Abbey

LARGE TEN-POINT STAR

Make 3

Ch 6, join with sl st in first ch.

Rnd 1: Ch 3 (count as dc), 14 dc in ring, join with sl st in 3rd ch of tch. *16 dc*

Rnd 2: Ch 4 (count as dc and ch 1), *dc in next st, ch 1; rep from * around, join with sl st in 3rd ch of tch. *15 ch-1 sps*

Rnd 3: Ch 5 (count as dc, and ch 2), *dc in next dc, ch 2: rep from * around, join with sl st in 3rd ch of tch. *15 ch-2 sps*

Rnd 4: *Ch 11, sl st in 3rd ch from hk, ch 8, skip 2 dc, sc in next dc; rep from * around. *5 star points*

Rnd 5: Working behind Rnd 4 and placing new sts in Rnd 3, sl st in first 3 sts, sc in next ch-2 sp, *ch 11, sl st in 3rd ch from hk, ch 8, skip 2 ch-2 sps, sc in next ch-2 sp; rep from * around ending sl st in first sc. *5 star points*

Fasten off.

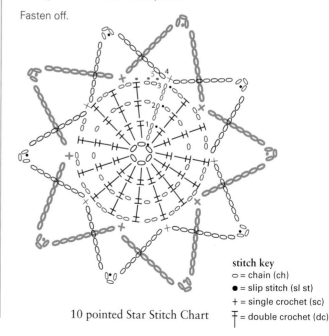

10 pointed Star Stitch Chart

stitch key
o = chain (ch)
● = slip stitch (sl st)
+ = single crochet (sc)
⊤ = double crochet (dc)

FINISHING

Join star points (see Assembly Diagram) by whipstitching star points tog using yarn tails. Weave in ends, apply small amount of fabric glue to yarn tail ends to secure. Spritz block to finished size.

Gazing At Stars with Edmund Assembly Diagram

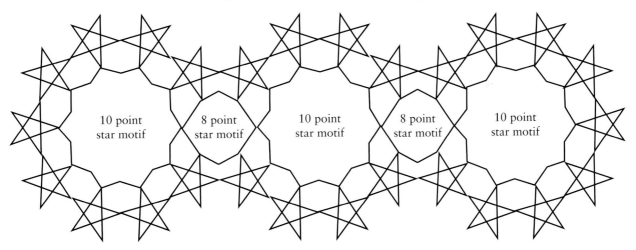

10 point star motif   8 point star motif   10 point star motif   8 point star motif   10 point star motif

Jane Austen mentions white gowns throughout several of her novels and letters. Why white? The white gown was the Regency's equivalent to today's black—a color always elegant, always in style and always in season. As white showed wear more quickly and noticeably than other Regency colors, a white dress also signified means and leisure.

❧ CATHERINE'S CLOAK ❧

SKILL LEVEL

MATERIALS

Classic Elite *Moorland* (42% fine merino wool, 23% baby alpaca, 19% mohair, 16% acrylic; 147 yds/135 m; dk weight #3 light): #2504 misty morning 12 (13, 14, 16, 17, 19) skeins

F-5 (3.75 mm) hk or size needed to obtain correct gauge

G-6 (4 mm) hk

5 Dill #450061 buttons, 70 mm

Stitcher's Kit (see page 187)

GAUGE

8 clusters and 8 rows in Catherine's cluster st patt = 4" (10 cm) with smaller hook.

FINISHED SIZES

XS (S, M, L, 1X, 2X) has hem circumference of 52 (55, 59, 62, 66, 68)"/132 (140, 150, 157.5, 167.5, 173) cm and length of 28 (29, 30, 31, 32, 33)"/71 (74, 76, 79, 81.5, 84) cm

STITCH GUIDE

View an online video demonstrating how to create this stitch pattern at: www.stitchscene.com/tutorials

Catherine Moreland loved gothic romance novels—intense tales of dimly lit chambers cloaked in mystery. This mantle is the perfect companion for secrets unveiled on stormy nights. The textured stitches create a soft halo that is opaque enough to chase the cold away, yet light enough to drape flatteringly about you. Oversized carved buttons bridge the time between then and now, making this a thoroughly modern cloak to wear on your chilliest of adventures.

CLUSTER STITCH

Yo, insert hk in st, yo and draw through st, yo and draw through 2 lps on hk, *yo, insert hk in same st, yo and draw through st, yo and draw through 2 lps on hk; rep from * once more, yo and draw through all 4 lps on hk.

BEG CLUSTER STITCH

Ch 3 (count as dc), yo, insert hk in first st, yo and draw through st, yo and draw through 2 lps on hk, yo, insert hk in same st, yo and draw through st, yo and draw through 2 lps on hk, yo and draw through all 3 lps on hk.

CATHERINE'S CLUSTER STITCH PATTERN

See chart page 154.

Foundation ch is multiple of 2 + 2.

Row 1 (WS): Yo, insert hk in first st, yo and draw through, yo and draw through 2 lps on hk, yo, insert hk in same st, yo and draw through, yo and draw through 2 lps on hk, yo and draw through all 3 lps on hk—beg cluster made, *skip 1 ch, (yo, insert hk in st, yo and draw through st, yo and draw through 2 lps on hk, **yo, insert hk in same st, yo and draw through st, yo

and draw through 2 lps on hk; rep from ** once more, yo and draw through all 4 lps on hk—cluster made; rep from * across ending with cluster in last ch, turn.

Row 2 (RS): Ch 1 (do not count as st), sc in first cluster, 2 sc in each cluster to last cluster, sc in last cluster, turn.

Row 3: Beg cluster in first st, *skip 1 sc, cluster in next sc; rep from * across, turn.

Rep Rows 2–3 for st patt.

Notes: Ch 1 at beg of row does not count as st throughout. Move all markers up to each new row as encountered.

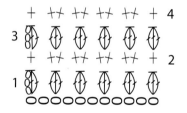

Catherine's Cluster Stitch Pattern Chart

stitch key
○ = chain (ch)
+ = single crochet (sc)
⬧ = double crochet cluster

CAPE

Ch 106 (110, 114, 118, 122, 126).

Row 1 (WS): Yo, insert hook in 4th ch from hook, yo, draw yarn through st, yo and draw through 2 loops on hook, yo,

insert hook in same st, yo and draw yarn through st, yo and draw through 2 lps on hook, yo and draw through all 3 loops on hook—beg cluster made, *skip 1 ch, cluster (see page 152) in next ch; rep from * across ending with cluster in last ch, turn. *52 (54, 56, 58, 60, 62) clusters*

Pm in foll sts:

XS: 13, 22, 30, 39;

S: 14, 23, 31, 40;

M: 14, 23, 33, 42;

L: 15, 24, 34, 43;

1X: 15, 25, 35, 45;

2X: 16, 26, 36, 46.

Row 2 and all RS Rows: Ch 1, sc in first cluster, 2 sc in each cluster to last cluster, sc in last cluster, turn. *102 (106, 110, 114, 118, 122) sts*

Row 3 (inc row): Beg cluster in first sc, *† skip 1 sc, cluster in next sc†, rep from † across to marked st, (cluster in marked st, cluster in next sc)—inc made; rep from * for 3 times; rep from † to † across, turn. *56 (58, 60, 62, 64, 66) clusters (beg cluster counted as cluster throughout)*

Rows 4–11: Rep Rows 2 and 3. *72 (74, 76, 78, 80, 82) clusters*

Row 13: Beg cluster in first sc, *skip 1 sc, cluster in next sc; rep from * across, turn.

Row 15: Rep Row 3. *76 (78, 80, 82, 84, 86) clusters*

Rows 16–19: Work even in established st patt for 3 rows; then

work inc row (Rep Rows 12–15). *80 (82, 84, 86, 88, 90) clusters*

Row 21: Rep Row 13 (13, 13, 3, 3, 3). *80 (82, 84, 90, 92, 94) clusters*

Rows 23–24: Rep Row 3; then work RS row in established st patt once. *84 (86, 88, 94, 96, 98) clusters*

RIGHT FRONT ARM OPENING

Row 25 (WS): Beg cluster in first sc, *skip 1 sc, cluster in next sc; rep from * for 8 (8, 9, 9, 11, 11) times, turn. *9 (9, 10, 10, 11, 11) clusters*

Next 14 Rows: Work even in established st patt.

Fasten off.

LEFT FRONT ARMHOLE OPENING

Join yarn to 17 (17, 19, 19, 21, 21) sc from left edge.

Row 25 (WS): Beg cluster in first sc, *skip 1 sc, cluster in next st; rep from * across, turn. *9 (9, 10, 10, 11, 11) clusters*

Next 14 Rows: Work even in established st patt.

Fasten off.

BACK

Join yarn to Row 24.

Row 25 (WS): Beg cluster in top of same Row 24 st as closest st for Right Front Armhole, *skip 1 sc, cluster in next sc; rep from * across unworked sts, cluster in top of same

"My cloak is come home. I like it very much, and can now exclaim with delight . . . This is what I have been looking for these three years."

—Jane Austen in a letter dated June 2, 1799

Row 24 st as worked for Left Front Armhole Opening, turn. *68 (70, 70, 76, 76, 78) clusters*

Row 27 (inc row): Beg cluster in first sc, *† skip 1 sc, cluster in next sc†, rep from † across to marked st, (cluster in marked st, cluster in next sc)—inc made; rep from * for 3 times; rep from † to † across, turn. *72 (74, 74, 80, 80, 82) clusters*

Rows 28–32: Work even in established st patt.

Row 33: Rep Row 27. *76 (78, 78, 84, 84, 86) clusters*

Rows 34–37: Rep Rows 30–33. *80 (82, 82, 88, 88, 90) clusters*

XS, S, M, L Only

Next 2 Rows: Work even in established st patt.

1X, 2X Only

Row 39: Rep Row 27. *(92, 94) clusters*

All Sizes

Fasten off.

JOINING FRONTS TO BACK

Join yarn to right front.

Row 40 (RS): Right Front: Ch 1, sc in first cluster, 2 sc in each of next 8 (8, 9, 9, 10, 10) clusters; place RS back underneath right front;

Overlap: sc in each of next 2 sts AT SAME TIME working through both layers;

Back: 2 sc in each st across to last 2 sts; place RS of left front on top of RS of back; rep Overlap; cont with 2 sc in each rem st across to last cluster, sc in cluster. *190 (194, 198, 210, 222, 226) sc*

Row 41: Beg cluster in first sc, *skip 1 sc, cluster in next sc; rep from * across, turn. *96 (98, 100, 106, 112, 114) clusters*

Row 43, (inc row): Beg cluster in first sc, *† skip 1 sc, cluster in next sc†, rep from † across to marked st, (cluster in marked st, cluster in next sc)—inc made; rep from * for 3 times; rep from † to † across, turn. *100 (102, 104, 110, 116, 118) clusters*

Row 45: Ch 3, beg cluster st in first sc, *(skip 1 sc, cluster st in next sc); rep from * across, turn.

XS, S Only

Next 3 (1) Rows: Work even in established st patt.

S, M, L, 1X, 2X Only

Next (2, 2, 2, 6, 6) Rows: Work in established st patt, working inc every WS row for (1, 1, 1, 3, 3) time, turn. *(106, 108, 114, 128, 130) clusters*

M, L, 2X Only

Next 4 Rows: Work even in established st patt for 3 rows; then inc on next row. *(112, 118, 134) clusters*

S, M, L, 1X, 2X Only

Next (3, 1, 3, 5, 3) Rows: Work even in established st patt.

All sizes

Fasten off.

NECKBAND

With larger hk, join yarn to neck edge and work 1 row of evenly spaced sc. Work even in sc for 10 more rows.

HEM BAND

Rep Neckband.

LEFT FRONT BAND

With larger hk and RS facing, join yarn to right side edge (side of Neckband) and work 87 (90, 93, 96, 99, 102) evenly spaced sc along edge. Work even in sc for 10 more rows.

Fasten off.

RIGHT FRONT BAND

Join yarn to hem and rep Left Front Band until 9 rows complete.

Row 10: Ch 1, sc in first 7 (10, 8, 6, 9, 7) sc, *ch 5, skip 5 sc, sc in next 11 (11, 12, 13, 13, 14) sts; rep from * for 4 times, sc across, turn.

Row 11: Ch 1, sc across.

Fasten off.

FINISHING

Sew buttons along center of Left Band using buttonholes on Right Front Band as placement guides. Weave in ends. Steam block, noting that schematic measurements do not include bands, so adjust pieces accordingly.

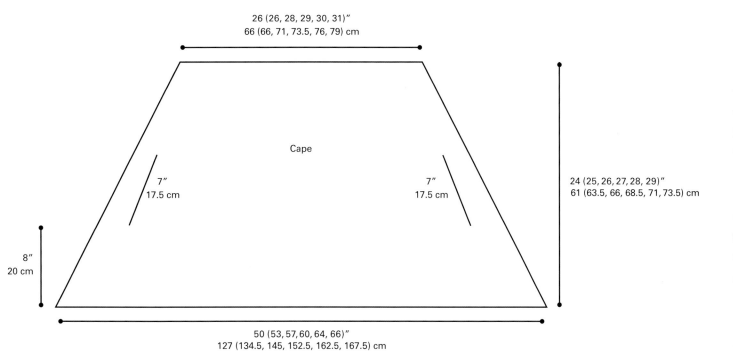

26 (26, 28, 29, 30, 31)"
66 (66, 71, 73.5, 76, 79) cm

Cape

7"
17.5 cm

7"
17.5 cm

24 (25, 26, 27, 28, 29)"
61 (63.5, 66, 68.5, 71, 73.5) cm

8"
20 cm

50 (53, 57, 60, 64, 66)"
127 (134.5, 145, 152.5, 162.5, 167.5) cm

Note: Schematics show measurements without 2" (5 cm) band at hem, neck, and front centers

CHAPTER 6

The Young Olive Branch: Clothing for Children

"The rest of his letter
is only about his dear
Charlotte's situation,
and his expectation
of a young olive-branch."

—*Pride and Prejudice*

A sound erupted from Miss Austen that was so startlingly in its loudness, the ladies glanced at one another speculatively. Had it been a laugh? A cry?

Emma was the first to take action. "Come Anne," said Emma dropping her hook and the church gown she was working on for Isabella's youngest. "Let us rest our hands and renew our circulation by taking a short turn about the room." Anne stood and took her proffered arm. "We shall see what this is about, shall we not," I heard Emma murmur.

Catherine caught up with them both and slipped her arm through Anne's free one. "I always fear Miss Austen has gone quite mad when she becomes like this," said Catherine.

"That is unlikely," said Anne. "She is more apt to write one of us to become so."

Catherine's eyes widened. "Truly? Which one of us do you think she might?"

"No, no" Emma reassured the young girl, "Anne was only mocking. Our Miss Austen writes nothing as sinister as that Miss Radcliffe's work to which you are so endeared. Yet my curiosity cannot help but become piqued by Miss Austen's behavior."

Emma shortened her stride and slowed their walk to a near stand as they approached the table at which Miss Austen was writing. As they walked past, the three strained their necks in as discreet a fashion as one could strain one's neck to see what fate Miss Austen was creating and to whom it would befall.

Once they had come full circle around the room, they were quickly joined by the others.

"Did you see what has her in such a state?" asked Jane, hoping that Bingley was finally proposing.

"I spied the word 'marriage'," Emma shared, confidently earning a smile from Jane.

"And I Mr. Collins" added Anne, to which Jane's smile faltered.

Marianne gasped loudly. "Someone is to marry Mr. Collins? Did you spy who, Catherine?"

"Shhhh!" they all hushed, their eyes turning to see if Miss Austen had heard.

"Did you see who?" repeated Elizabeth to Catherine.

Catherine shook her head no. "And I cannot begin to guess who would be so horrifically sensible?"

All eyes turned to Elinor. "Well do not look to me" said Elinor. "I, very fortunately, am not in that story."

"Oh Lizzy," moaned Jane, joining her hand in her sister's. "It is either to be you or me, I fear."

"Do not think it is me. I have already rejected him once . . ." she stammered. "It could be you, dear sister." Yet Elizabeth recognized the foolishness of her words as soon as they were spoken. Still, one could hope.

"I refuse. I have adamantly refused," Elizabeth said, stabbing her finger toward Miss Austen, "And she knows that! I would sooner live in the wilderness like a beast of the field than marry that odious man."

"But I have it on very good authority," Elinor said, recollecting her earlier conversation with Mr. Collins, "that the young woman who is so fortuitous to become his wife will have some very fine shelves in her closet indeed. You may want to reconsider Lizzy," she added, with eyes twinkling.

SKILL LEVEL

MATERIALS

Cascade *Ultra Pima* (100% pima cotton;
220 yds/202 m; dk weight #3 light):
#3728 white 6 (7, 8) skeins

F-5 (3.75 mm) hk or size needed to
obtain correct gauge

3 white frog closures 2½″ (6 cm)

Stitcher's Kit (see page 187)

GAUGE

8 berries and 18 rows in Uneven Berry
Stitch Pattern = 4″ (10 cm)

FINISHED SIZES

Newborn (6 months, 12 months) has
chest circumference of 19 (20½, 21¼)″/
48.5 (52, 54) cm

STITCH GUIDE

View an online video demonstrating
how to create this stitch pattern
at: www.stitchscene.com/tutorials

*I*nspired by Jane's childhood home, this beautiful infant church gown will rise to heirloom stature. The fine stitching of the pima cotton gives this design its unique satin softness. Tasteful, timeless, and loaded with texture, it works for either a boy or a girl, allowing it to be handed down from generation to generation. Frog closures provide a distinctive finishing touch.

UNEVEN BERRY STITCH PATTERN

See chart page 162.

Foundation ch is multiple of 2 +1.

Note: Foundation is just multiple of 2 when worked in rnd.

Row 1: Sc in 3rd ch from hk, sc in each ch across, turn.

Row 2 (WS): Ch 1 (count as first sl st), skip first st, *yo and insert hk in next st, yo and draw through lp, yo and draw through first lp on hk, yo and insert hk in same st, yo and draw through lp, yo and draw through all 5 lps on hk, ch 1 to secure (do not count as st)—(berry made), sl st in next st; rep from * across ending sl st in tch, turn.

Row 3: Ch 1 (count as sc), *sl st in next berry, sc in next sl st; rep from * across, turn.

Row 4: Ch 1 (count as berry), sl st in sl st, *berry in next sc, sl st in next sl st; rep from * to last st, sl st in last st, turn.

Row 5: Ch 1 (count as sl st), *sc in next sl st, sl st in next berry; rep from * across, turn.

Rep Rows 2–5 for st patt.

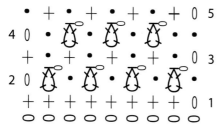

Uneven Berry Stitch Pattern Chart

stitch key
○ = chain (ch)
● = slip stitch (sl st)
+ = single crochet (sc)
⊼ = berry stitch

SPLIT SINGLE CROCHET STITCH (ssc)

Work as for basic sc EXCEPT start by inserting hk through work between 2 vertical strands of sc in previous row.

SPLIT SINGLE CROCHET DECREASE STITCH (ssc2tog)

Insert hk in st as for ssc, yo and draw through lp, insert hk in next st as for ssc, yo and draw through lp, yo and draw through all 3 lps on hk.

REVERSE SINGLE CROCHET STITCH (rev sc)

Working from left to right, insert hk in st to right, work sc (yo and draw through st, yo and draw through 2 lps on hk).

BODY

Note: Pm in tch to note beg of rnd being sure to move marker up with each new rnd.

Ch 114 (116, 116), taking care not to twist ch, join with sl st (do not count as st) in first ch.

Rnd 1: Ch 1 (do not count as st), sc in first and each ch around, join with sl st in tch, turn. *114 (116, 116) sts*

Rnd 2: Ch 1, sl st in next st *yo and insert hk in next st, yo and draw through lp, yo and draw through first lp on hk, yo and insert hk in same st, yo and draw through lp, yo and draw through all 5 lps on hk, ch 1 to secure—(berry made), sl st in next st; rep from * around to last st, berry in last st, sl st in tch, turn. *57 (58, 58) berries*

Rnd 3: Ch 1, *sl st in next berry, sc in next sl st; rep from * around, join with sl st in tch, turn.

Rnd 4: Ch 1, *berry in next sc, sl st in next sl st; rep from around, join with sl st in tch, turn.

Rnd 5: Ch 1, *sc in next sl st, sl st in next berry; rep from * across, join with sl st in tch, turn.

Rnds 6–8: Rep Rnds 2–4.

Rnd 9: Ch 1, skip next sl st—dec made, *sl st in next berry, sc in next sl st; rep from * across to last 2 sts, sc in next sl st, skip last berry—dec made, join with sl st in first ch, turn. *112 (114, 114) sts for 55 (56, 56) berries in next row*

Rnds 10–11: Rep Rnds 4–5.

Rnds 12–14: Rep Rnds 2–4.

Rnds 15–44 (15–44, 15–38): Rep Rnds 9–14 for 5 (5, 4) times. *45 (46, 48) berries*

Next 2 Rnds: Rep Rows 4-5.

Next 40 (44, 56) Rnds: Rep Rows Rnds 2–5 for 10 (11, 14) times.

All Sizes

Rnd 87 (91, 97): Ch 1, sc around. *90 (92, 96) sts*

Fasten off.

CHEST

With RS of body facing, join yarn to 44th st to the left of marker, turn.

Row 1 (short row): Ch 1 (do not count as st), ssc (see page 162) around, do not join, turn. *88 (92, 96) sts*

Remove marker. Work even (Rep Row 1) for 9 (11, 13) more times.

LEFT FRONT

Note: Do not count ch 1 at beg of each row as st.

ARMHOLE SHAPING

Row 11 (13, 15) (short row): Ch 1, ssc in first 22 (23, 24) sts, turn.

Row 12 (14, 16): Ch 1, ssc2tog—dec made at side seam (see page 162), ssc across, turn. *21 (22, 23) sts*

Row 13 (15, 17): Ch 1, ssc across leaving last st unworked, turn. *20 (21, 22) sts*

Rows 14 (16, 18): Ch 1, ssc across, turn.

Row 15 (17, 19): Ch 1, ssc across leaving last st unworked, turn. *19 (20, 21) sts*

Next 8 (10, 12) Rows: Ch 1, ssc across, turn.

NECKLINE SHAPING

Row 24 (28, 32): Ch 1, ssc across leaving last 2 sts unworked, turn. *17 (18, 19) sts*

Next Row: Ch 1, ssc2tog, ssc across, turn. *16 (17, 18) sts*

Next 2 Rows: Rep last 2 rows. *13 (14, 15) sts*

12 Months Only

Next Row: Ch 1, ssc across leaving last st unworked. *(14 sts)*

All Sizes

Fasten off.

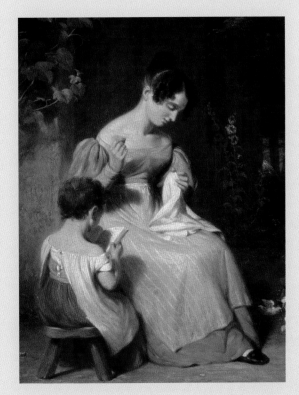

How well do you know the younger characters in Jane Austen's novels?

1. What is the name of the youngest Dashwood sister?

2. Name Fanny's youngest sister, who eventually moved to Mansfield Park.

3. Which heroine did not have any younger siblings?

Find out on page 203.

RIGHT FRONT

With RS facing and working in Chest Row 10 (12, 14), join yarn to first unworked st to left of Left Front center. Rep Left Front, working first st in same st as join.

BACK

Note: Do not count ch 1 at beg of each row as st.

With RS facing and working in Chest Row 10 (12, 14), join yarn in next unworked st to left of Right Front.

Row 1: Ch 1, ssc in same st as join and every unworked st across, turn. *46 (46, 48) sts*

Rows 2–3: Ch 1, ssc2tog, sc across ending ssc2tog, turn. *42 (42, 44) sts*

Row 4: Ch 1, ssc across, turn.

Row 5: Rep Row 2. *40 (40, 42) sts*

Newborn Only

Row 6: Rep Row 2. *38 sts*

All Sizes

Next 10 (13, 16) Rows: Rep Row 3.

SLEEVE

Make 2

Ch 33 (37, 39).

Row 1: Sc in 2nd ch from hk, sc in each ch across, turn. *32 (36, 38) sts*

Row 2: Ch 1 (count as sl st), skip first st, *berry in next st, sl st in next st; rep from * across ending last sl st in tch, turn. *16 (18, 19) berries*

Row 3: Ch 1 (count as sc), *sl st in next berry, sc in next sl st; rep from * across, turn.

Row 4: Ch 1 (count as berry), sl st in sl st, *berry in next sc, sl st in next sl st; rep from * to last st, sl st in tch, turn.

Row 5: Ch 1 (count as sl st), *sc in next sl st, sl st in next berry; rep from * across, turn.

Rows 6–8: Rep Rows 2–4.

Row 9: Ch 1, skip first 2 sts, *sl st in berry, sc in sl st; rep from * across leaving last 2 sts (sl st and ch-1 tch) unworked, turn. *28 (32, 34) sts*

Row 10: Ch 1 (count as sl st), skip first sl st, *berry in next sc, sl st in next sl st; rep from * across to last sl st and tch, sl st in tch, turn. *13 (15, 16) berries*

Row 11: Rep Row 3, ending last sc in tch. Fasten off.

FINISHING

Steam block. Sew shoulder and underarm seams. Set in sleeves. With RS facing, join yarn to bottom of left front at center of neckline, work 1 row rev sc (see page 162) up left neckline, around back neckline and down right front, join with a sl st to first rev sc.

With WS facing, work 1 row of (berry, sl st) around hemline and cuffs being sure to space berries between current berries on crocheted fabric. Along front neckline, sew evenly spaced frog closures, taking care to slightly overlap right front over left when positioning.

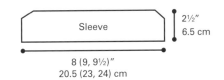

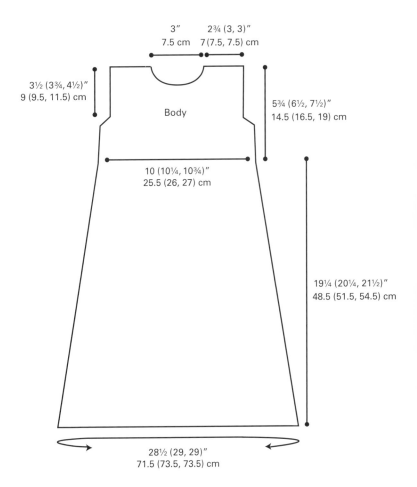

SKILL LEVEL

MATERIALS

Knit Picks *City Tweed* DK (55% merino wool, 25% superfine alpaca, 20% donegal tweed; 123 yds / 110 m; dk weight #3 light): #25438 porpoise (MC) 2 skeins for hat and 2 skeins for muff; #24550 tabby (CC1) 1 skein for hat and muff

H-8 (5 mm) hk or size needed to obtain correct gauge

⅜" (10 mm) velvet ribbon, 30" (76 cm) long

Bowl with 18" (46 cm) circumference

Masking tape

Stitcher's Kit (see page 187)

GAUGE

11 sc and 14 rows = 4" (10 cm)

FINISHED SIZES

Hat circumference of 18" (45.7 cm) fits most. Hat can be made larger by felting less and alternatively, smaller by felting stitches more. Muff has a circumference of 8¼" (21 cm) excluding flared ends, and length of 13½" (34 cm).

STITCH GUIDE

View an online video demonstrating how to create this stitch pattern at: www.stitchscene.com/tutorials

*I*ntroduce the young girl in your life to the fashionable pleasures of Austen with this felted hat and muff set. She is sure to be everyone's darling while wearing this ensemble. Worked in a yarn laced with donegal tweed to create a beautiful flecked felt, there is stunning depth to the hat not often found in felted fabrics. Trimmed with flowers and brown velvet ribbon, nothing could be simpler, or sweeter.

FOUNDATION SINGLE CROCHET STITCH (fsc)

Ch 2, insert hk in 2nd ch from hk, yarn over hk and draw through lp, yarn over hk and draw through first lp on hk, yarn over hk and draw through 2 lps on hk–1 fsc made, *insert hk under 2 lps of ch made at base of previous st, yarn over hk and draw through lp, yarn over hk and draw through first lp on hk, yarn over hk and draw through 2 lps on hk; rep from * for desired number of foundation sts.

SINGLE CROCHET DECREASE STITCH (sc2tog)

Insert hk in st, yo and draw through lp, insert hk in next st, yo and draw through lp, yo and draw through all 3 lps on hk.

HAT BODY

Note: Pm to note beg of each rnd being sure to move marker up with each row.

With MC, ch 4, join with sl st in first ch.

Rnd 1: 6 sc in ring.

Rnd 2: 2 sc in each sc around. *12 sts*

Rnd 3: *Sc in next 1 sc, 2 sc in next sc—inc made; rep from * around. *18 sts.*

Rnd 4: *Sc in next 2 sc, 2 sc in next sc; rep from * around. *24 sts.*

Rnd 5: *Sc in next 3 sc, 2 sc in next sc; rep from * around. *30 sts.*

Rnd 6: *Sc in next 4 sc, 2 sc in next sc; rep from * around. *36 sts.*

Rnd 7: *Sc in next 5 sc, 2 sc in next sc; rep from * around. *42 sts.*

Next 18 Rnds: Work in sc AT SAME TIME for every new rnd work even for 1 more st before working each inc (2 sc in next sc). *150 sts*

Rnd 26: *Sc in next 23 sts, sc2tog (see page 166)—dec made; rep from * around. *144 sts*

Rnd 27: *Sc in next 22 sts, sc2tog; rep from * around. *138 sts*

Next 10 Rnds: Work in sc AT SAME TIME for every new rnd work even for 1 less st before working each dec. *78 sts*

Next 4 Rnds: Sc around.

Rnd 42: *Sc flo in next 12 sc, 2 sc flo in next sc; rep from * around. *84 sts*

Rnd 43: *Sc flo in next 13 sc, 2 sc flo in next sc; rep from * around. *90 sts*

Rnd 44: *Sc in next 14 sc, 2 sc in next sc; rep from * around. *96 sts*

Rnd 45: *Sc in next 15 sc, 2 sc in next sc; rep from * around. *102 sts*

Next 4 Rnds (inc rnds): Work in sc AT SAME TIME for every new rnd work even for 1 more st before working each inc (2 sc in next sc). *126 sts*

EDGING

Rnd 50: With CC1, *sc in next 20 sc, 2 sc in next sc; rep from * around. *132 sts*

Fasten off. Loosely knot tog beg tail at center of RS of hat to small amount CC1 several times.

ROLLED FLOWER FABRIC

With MC, ch 35.

Row 1: Sc in 2nd ch from hk and in each ch across, turn. *34 sts*

Next 11 rnds: Ch 1, sc across, turn. Fasten off.

Join CC1 and work evenly spaced sc around all 4 edges and working 3 sc in each corner. Fasten off.

MUFF

Note: Ch 1 at beg of rnds does not count as st.

Rnd 1: In MC, 78 fsc (see page 166), join with sl st in first fsc, pm (do not move up every rnd), turn. *78 sts*

Rnds 2–15: Ch 1, sc around, join with sl st in first sc, turn.

Rnd 16 (inc rnd): Ch 1, 2 sc in each sc around, join with sl st in first sc, turn. *156 sts*

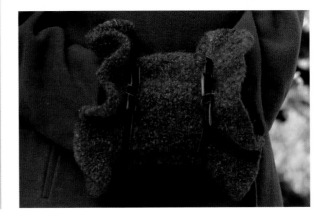

Next 4 Rnds: Ch 1, sc around, join with sl st in first sc, turn. Fasten off MC.

Rnd 21: With CC1, ch 1, sc around, join with sl st in first sc. Fasten off.

Working on opposite side of foundation ch, join MC at marker. Remove marker.

Rep Rows 16–21.

FELTING

Weave in ends. Felt (see page 197) all pieces until stitches are tight and indiscernible. Block hat over bowl having approximately same circumference as desired finished hat size: turn bowl upside down and determine place where bowl is desired circumference of hat. Mark with tape to use as guideline for positioning hat.

Shape hat. Cut knotted tails in center of hat to ½" (13 mm). Let all pieces dry completely. Neatly finish felted hat, muff, and rolled flower fabric by brushing with sweater comb and snipping loose tidbits off surface with scissors. Place 2 Leaf and 1 long Flower shapes layout on felted fabric as shown and cut. Roll triangle into flower. Sew velvet ribbon around center edges of muff and add bow.

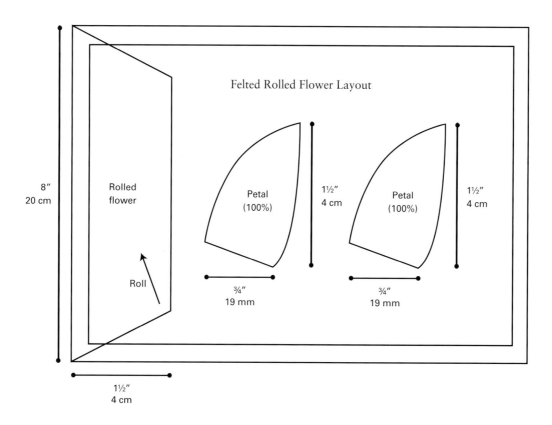

Felted Rolled Flower Layout

8"
20 cm

Rolled flower

Roll

Petal (100%)

1½"
4 cm

¾"
19 mm

Petal (100%)

1½"
4 cm

¾"
19 mm

1½"
4 cm

SKILL LEVEL

MATERIALS

KnitPicks *CotLin* (70% tanguis cotton, 30% linen; 123 yds / 113 m; dk weight #3 light): #23996 moroccan red (MC) 5 (6, 7) skeins; 1 skein each of #24137 crème brulee (CC1), #24462 sprout (CC2), #24134 swan (CC3), #24459 surf (CC4), #24460 clementine (CC5)

F-5 (3.75 mm) hk or size needed to obtain correct gauge

Stitcher's Kit (see page 187)

GAUGE

17 sts and 20 rows worked in crunch st patt = 4" (10 cm)

FINISHED SIZES

Girl's 6 (8, 10) / S (M, L) has chest circumference of 23½ (26½, 27½)"/ 60 (67.5, 70) cm and armhole depth of 7¼ (7¾, 8¼)"/ 18.5 (19.75, 21) cm

STITCH GUIDE

View an online video demonstrating how to create this stitch pattern at: www.stitchscene.com / tutorials

This playful design, worked in a soft cotton linen blend, is picture-perfect for everything from school days to garden party plays. The knee-length dress features a scoop neckline and an easy empire silhouette. Rounded patch pockets designed to hold tiny treasures and vibrant colors enliven even the most routine days for your precious poppet.

CRUNCH STITCH PATTERN

Foundation ch is multiple of 2 + 1.

Row 1: Sc in 2nd ch from hk, sl st in next st, *sc in next st, sl next st; rep from * across, turn.

Row 2: Ch 1, sc in first sl st, sl st in next sc, *sc in next sl st, sl st in next sc; rep from * across, turn.

Rep Row 2 for st patt.

Note: Ch 1 and/or sl st(s) at beg of rows do not count as st(s) throughout this patt.

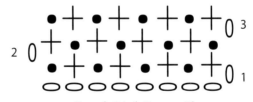

Crunch Stitch Pattern Chart

stitch key
○ = chain (ch)
● = slip stitch (sl st)
+ = single crochet (sc)

FRONT

With CC1, ch 75 (83, 87). Fasten off CC1.

Row 1 (RS): With CC2, sc in 2nd ch from hk, sl st in next ch, *sc in next ch, sl st in next st; rep from * across, turn. *74 (82, 86) sts* Fasten off CC2.

Row 2: With CC1, ch 1, sc in first sl st, sl st in next sc, *sc in next sl st, sl st in next sc; rep from * across, turn. Fasten off CC1.

Rows 3–10: Rep Row 2 changing col as foll: 1 row CC3, 2 rows CC1, one row each of CC4, CC5, CC2, CC3, then CC1. Fasten off each CC when no longer worked.

Join MC.

Row 11 (dec row): Ch 1, skip first st, work in established st patt (sc, sl st OR sl st, sc—see page 171) across leaving last st unworked, turn. *72 (80, 84) sts*

Next 4 (5, 5) Rows: Ch 1, work in established st patt across, turn.

Next Row: Rep Row 11. *70 (78, 82) sts*

Next 63 (80, 88) Rows: Work in established st patt with dec row (rep Row 11) every 7th (8th, 8th) row for 9 (10, 11) times. *52 (58, 60) sts*

Next 2 Rows: Work in established st patt across, turn.

ARMHOLE SHAPING

Row 82 (100, 108): Sl st in first 3 (3, 2) sts, work in established st patt across leaving last 3 (3, 2) sts unworked, turn. *46 (52, 56) sts*

Size S Only

Next 4 Rows: Ch 1, work in established st patt across, turn.

Size M Only

Next Row: Ch 1, skip first st, work in established st patt across leaving last st unworked, turn. *(50) sts*

Next 3 Rows: Ch 1, work in established st patt across, turn.

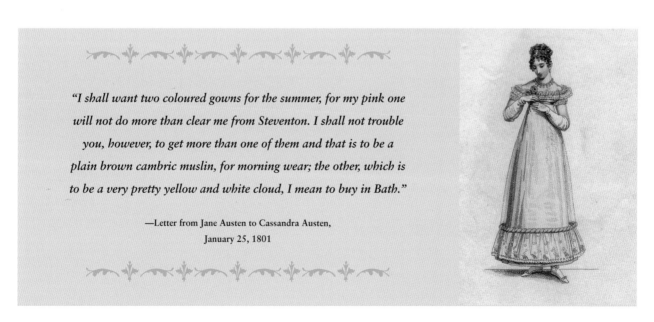

"I shall want two coloured gowns for the summer, for my pink one will not do more than clear me from Steventon. I shall not trouble you, however, to get more than one of them and that is to be a plain brown cambric muslin, for morning wear; the other, which is to be a very pretty yellow and white cloud, I mean to buy in Bath."

—Letter from Jane Austen to Cassandra Austen,
January 25, 1801

Next Row (dec row): Ch 1, skip first st, work in established st patt across leaving last st unworked, turn. *(54) sts*

Next Row: Ch 1, work in established st patt across, turn.

Next Row: Rep dec row. *(52) sts*

Next Row: Ch 1, work in established st patt across, turn.

All sizes

Row 87 (105, 113) (dec row): Ch 1, skip first st, work in established st patt across leaving last st unworked, turn. *44 (48, 50) sts*

Next 6 (8, 8) Rows: Work in established st patt working dec row every 2nd row. *38 (42, 44) sts*

Row 94 (114, 122): Rep dec row. *36 (40, 42) sts*

Next 7 (5, 5) Rows: Ch 1, work in established st patt across, turn.

FIRST SHOULDER SHAPING

Row 102 (120, 128) (short row): Ch 1, work in established st patt across first 6 sts, turn.

Next 31 (37, 41) Rows: Rep last row. Fasten off.

OPPOSITE SHOULDER SHAPING

With RS facing, join MC to outer edge of last row of Armhole Shaping and rep First Shoulder Shaping.

BACK

Rep Front to end of Armhole Shaping. Fasten off.

POCKETS

Make 2

With MC, ch 9.

Row 1: Hdc in 2nd ch from hk (count as hdc) and in each ch across, turn. *8 sts*

Row 2: Ch 1, 2 hdc in first st, hdc across ending 2 hdc in last st, turn. *10 sts*

Rows 3–5: Rep Row 2. *16 sts*

Row 6: Ch 1, hdc across, turn. Fasten off MC.

Join CC3.

Row 7: Ch 1, sc in first st, sl st in next st, *sc in next st, sl st in next st; rep from * across, turn. Fasten off CC3.

Rows 8–12: Rep Row 7 starting with CC4 and changing col every row as foll: CC5, CC2, CC3, CC1. Fasten off each col as row is completed.

FINISHING

Weave in ends. Steam block to schematic measurements. Sew side seams taking care to line up col rows at hem. Sew front straps to back. Position bottom of each pocket 7" (17.5 cm) above hem, 3½" (9 cm) apart, sl st pockets in place.

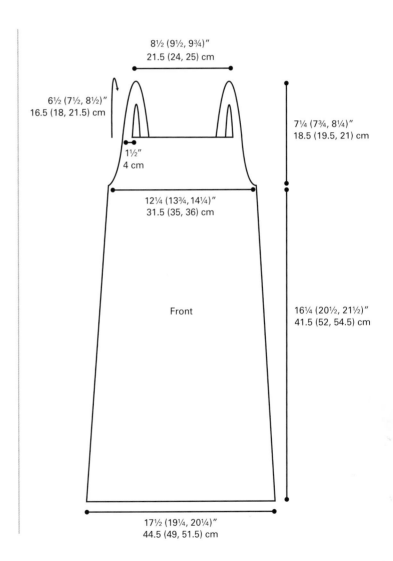

8½ (9½, 9¾)"
21.5 (24, 25) cm

6½ (7½, 8½)"
16.5 (18, 21.5) cm

7¼ (7¾, 8¼)"
18.5 (19.5, 21) cm

1½"
4 cm

12¼ (13¾, 14¼)"
31.5 (35, 36) cm

Front

16¼ (20½, 21½)"
41.5 (52, 54.5) cm

17½ (19¼, 20¼)"
44.5 (49, 51.5) cm

SKILL LEVEL

MATERIALS

Classic Elite *Moorland*, (42% fine merino wool, 23% baby alpaca, 19% mohair, 16% acrylic; 147 yds/135 m; dk weight #3 light): #2504 misty morning 4 (4, 5) skeins

G-6 (4 mm) hk or size needed to obtain correct gauge

Stitcher's Kit (see page 187)

GAUGE

3 clusters and 6 rows in Candy Cover Stitch Pattern = 4" (10 cm) after blocking

FINISHED SIZES

Girl's 4 (6, 8)/S (M, L) has waist circumference of 22¾ (24, 26¾)"/58 (61, 68) cm. Waist ties can be loosened as necessary to grow with child.

STITCH GUIDE

View an online video demonstrating how to create this stitch pattern at: www.stitchscene.com/tutorials

*S*he will be quite at ease whether at work or play wearing this comfortable apron dress. The pattern features a slanted block stitch that creates a scalloped hem she will adore. The ruffled halter and waist ties ensure a fit that will grow with her for some time. Shown in a traditional Regency color, if worked in a variegated yarn, it would make for exceptionally fun results. Pair over a comfortable shirt and leggings for a modern style she will thoroughly enjoy.

CANDY COVER STITCH PATTERN

Foundation ch is multiple of 4 +4

Row 1 (RS): 4 dc in 4th ch from hk, skip 3 ch—first cluster made, sc in next ch, *ch 2, 4 dc in same ch as sc, skip 3 ch, sc in next ch —cluster made; rep from * across, turn.

Row 2: Ch 5, 4 dc in 4th ch from hk, *skip 4 dc, sc between last skipped dc and next ch, ch 2, 4 dc in side of sc just worked; rep from * to last cluster, skip 4 dc, sc in next ch, turn.

Rep Row 2 for st patt.

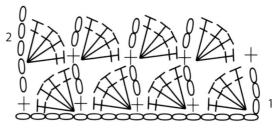

stitch key
○ = chain (ch)
+ = single crochet (sc)
Ŧ = double crochet (dc)

Candy Cover Stitch Pattern Chart

SKIRT

Ch 72 (76, 84).

Row 1 (RS): 4 dc in 4th ch from hk, skip 3 ch—first cluster made, sc in next ch, *ch 2, 4 dc in same ch as sc, skip 3 ch, sc in next ch —cluster made; rep from * across, turn. *17 (18, 20) clusters*

Row 2: Ch 5, 4 dc in 4th ch from hk, *skip 4 dc, sc between last skipped dc and next ch, ch 2, 4 dc in side of last sc worked; rep from * to last 4 dc cluster, skip 4 dc, sc in next ch, turn.

Next 15 (17, 21) Rows: Rep Row 2.

Fasten off.

FRONT PANEL

Ch 16 (20. 24).

SIDE ONE

Row 1 (RS): 4 dc in 4th ch from hk, skip 3 ch, sc in next ch, *ch 2, 4 dc in same ch as sc, skip 3 ch, sc in next ch; rep from * across, turn. *3 (4, 5) clusters*

Next 5 (7, 11) Rows: Work even in established st patt across, turn.

Fasten off.

SIDE TWO

Rotate work so foundation ch is at top. With RS is facing, join yarn to first foundation ch at upper right corner.

Row 1: Sc in first and each ch across, turn. *14 (18, 22) sts*

Row 2: Ch 1 (do not count as st), 2 sc flo in each sc across. *28 (36, 44) sts*

Fasten off.

HALTER TIE

Make 2

Ch 51 (58, 71).

SIDE ONE

Row 1: Sc in 2nd ch from hk and in each ch across, turn. *50 (57, 70) sts*

Row 2: Ch 1 (do not count as st), 2 sc flo in each sc across. *100 (114, 140) sts*

Fasten off.

SIDE TWO

Rotate work so foundation ch is at top. With RS is facing, join yarn to first foundation ch at right corner.

Row 1: Rep Row 2 of Side 1.

Fasten off.

WAIST TIE

Ch 185 (191, 197).

SIDE ONE

Row 1: Sc in 2nd ch from hk and in each ch across, turn.

184 (190, 196) sts

Row 2: Ch 1 (do not count as st), sc in each st across, turn.

Row 3: Ch 1 (do not count as st), sc in first 53 sts, 2 sc flo in next 78 (84, 90) sts, sc in each st across. *368 (380, 392) sts*

Fasten off.

SIDE TWO

Rotate work so foundation ch is at top. With RS facing join yarn to first foundation ch at right corner.

Row 1 (inc row): Rep Row 3 of Side 1.

Fasten off.

FINISHING

Steam block to schematic measurements, pinning ruffled edges neatly.

Place WS of Halter Tie against RS of Front Panel side edge. Whipstitch the pieces tog by working through back loops of Halter Tie Row 1 of Side 1 so ruffle hides stitching. Attach rem Halter Tie to opposite Front Panel edge.

Sew Waist Tie to top of skirt, again using available lps underneath ruffle of waist tie, making sure tie ends are same length on both sides of skirt. Center Front Panel underneath Waist Tie and sew.

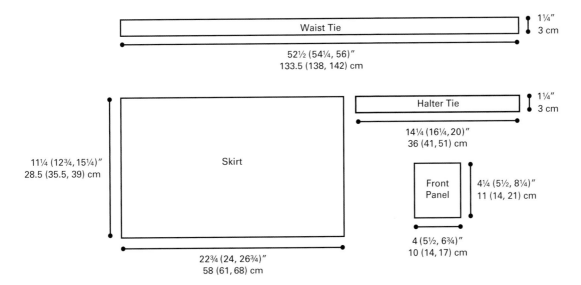

Waist Tie

1¼"
3 cm

52½ (54¼, 56)"
133.5 (138, 142) cm

Halter Tie

1¼"
3 cm

14¼ (16¼, 20)"
36 (41, 51) cm

Skirt

11¼ (12¾, 15¼)"
28.5 (35.5, 39) cm

Front Panel

4¼ (5½, 8¼)"
11 (14, 21) cm

22¾ (24, 26¾)"
58 (61, 68) cm

4 (5½, 6¾)"
10 (14, 17) cm

SKILL LEVEL

MATERIALS

Berroco *Comfort* (50% super fine nylon, 50% super fine acrylic; 210 yds / 193 m; worsted weight #4): #9717 Raspberry Coulis, Girl's Capelet: 2 (3, 3, 4) skeins, Doll's Capelet: 1 skein

G-6 (4 mm) hk or size needed to obtain correct gauge

8 (10, 12, 14) Tip-drilled teardrop beads

Stitcher's Kit (see page 187)

GAUGE

2 (7-LDC) fans and 4 rows = 4" (10 cm) in Peacock Stitch Pattern

FINISHED SIZES

Girl's 4 (6, 8, 10)/S (M, L, XL) Cape has neckline of 12¼ (16¼, 20¼, 24¼)"/31 (41, 51.5, 61.5) cm and length of 11 (11, 12, 13)"/28 (28, 30.5, 33) cm. Doll's Capelet to fit 18" (46 cm) doll.

STITCH GUIDE

View an online video demonstrating how to create this stitch pattern at: www.stitchscene.com/tutorials

*E*xploring the streets of Bath to find the best sweet shop, your little girl is sure to delight in this simple capelet designed to spice up any top or outfit she is wearing. The peacock stitch makes for easy increasing and she will note and appreciate a row of playful fringes with beaded accents. Quick and easy, you will enjoy making this design as much as she will enjoy receiving it. Make her even happier by stitching up the matching design for her 18" (46 cm) doll.

LONG DOUBLE CROCHET STITCH (ldc)

Yo, insert hk in next st and draw lp through st to ½" (1.25 cm) length, (yo and draw through 2 lps on hk) twice.

FRONT POST DOUBLE CROCHET STITCH (fpdc)

Yo hk, insert hk around post of specified stitch (from front to back and then back to front) in previous row, yo and draw lp through to back of post then to front of same st, complete as for double crochet: (yo and draw through 2 lps on hk) twice.

PEACOCK STITCH PATTERN

See chart page 182.

Foundation ch is 8 + 2.

Row 1: Sc in 2nd ch from hk, *skip 3 ch, 7 LDC in next ch, skip 3 ch, sc in next ch; rep from * across, turn.

Row 2: Ch 4, LDC in first sc, *ch 2, sc in 4th st of 7-LDC group, ch 2, 2 LDC in next sc; rep from * across, turn.

Row 3: Ch 1, *sc between 2 LDC, 7 LDC in next sc; rep from * across, sc between last 2 LDC and tch, turn.

Row 4: Ch 4, LDC in first sc, *ch 2, sc in 4th st of 7-LDC group, ch 2, 2 LDC in next sc; rep from * across, turn.

Rep Rows 3 and 4 for patt.

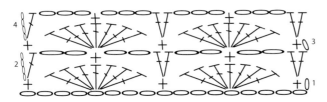

Peacock Stitch Pattern Chart
for Gauge Swatch

stitch key
○ = chain (ch)
+ = single crochet (sc)
⊤ = double crochet (dc)

BOW TIE STITCH PATTERN

Foundation ch is 7+ 8.

Row 1: Hdc in 2nd ch from hk (count as hdc) and each ch across, turn.

Row 2 (RS): Ch 1, sc in first 2 sts, *ch 4, skip next 4 hdc, sc in each of next 3 hdc; rep from * across to last two sts, sc in each of last 2 sts, turn.

Row 3: (Sl st in first st, ch 3—tch made, 4 dc, ch 2, 4 dc) in first ch-lp, *(4 dc, ch 2, 4 dc) in next ch-lp; rep from * across ending (4 dc, ch 2, 5 dc) in last ch-lp, turn.

Row 4: Ch 1, sc in first st, *ch 3, sc in ch-2 sp, (ch 15, sc) in same sp 3 times—bow tie made, ch 3, skip 4 dc, sc in next dc; rep from * across ending last sc in top of tch.

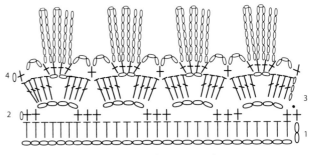

Bow-tie Stitch Pattern Chart

stitch key
○ = chain (ch)
● = slip stitch (sl st)
+ = single crochet (sc)
⊤ = half double crochet (hdc)
⊤̄ = double crochet (dc)

GIRL'S CAPE
TOP TIER

Note: Worked from neckline to hem.

Ch 44 (58, 72, 86).

Row 1: Hdc in 2nd ch from hk (count as hdc) and each ch across, turn. *43 (57, 71, 85) hdc*

Row 2 (RS): Ch 1, sc in first 2 sts, *ch 4, skip next 4 hdc, sc in each of next 3 hdc; rep from * across to last two sts, sc in last hdc and top of tch, turn. *6 (8, 10, 12) ch-4 lps*

Row 3: (Sl st in first st, ch 3—tch made, 4 dc, ch 2, 4 dc) in first ch-lp, *(4 dc, ch 2, 4 dc) in next ch-lp; rep from * across to last ch-lp, (4 dc, ch 2, 5 dc) in ch-lp, turn. *48 (64, 80, 96) dc*

Row 4: Ch 1, sc in first st, *ch 3, sc in ch-2 sp, (ch 15, sc) in same sp 3 times—bow tie made, ch 3, skip 4 dc, sc in next dc; rep from * across ending last sc in top of tch.

Fasten off.

MIDDLE TIER

Started underneath—and working into—Top Tier. With WS facing, join yarn to top of tch at beg of Row 3.

Row 1: Ch 2 (count as hdc), hdc flo in each Top Tier dc across Row 3, turn. *48 (64, 80, 96) hdc*

Row 2: Ch 1, sc in first hdc, *skip 3 sts, 7 LDC (see page 180) in next st, skip 3 sts, sc in next st; rep from * across, turn. *49 (65, 81, 97) hdc or 6 (8, 10, 12) fans*

Row 3: Ch 4, LDC in same st, *ch 2, sc in 4th LDC of 7-LDC group, ch 2, 2 LDC in next sc; rep from * across, turn.

Row 4: Ch 1, *sc between 2 LDC, 7 LDC in next sc; rep from * across, sc between last 2 LDC and tch, turn.

Row 5: Rep Row 3.

Row 6: Ch 1, *sc between 2 LDC, 9 LDC in next sc; rep from * across, sc between last LDC and tch, turn.

Row 7: Ch 4, LDC in first sc, *ch 3, sc in 5th st of 9-LDC group, ch 3, 2 LDC in next sc; rep from * across, turn.

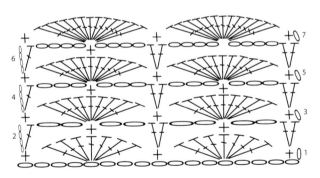

Peacock Stitch Pattern Chart

stitch key
o = chain (ch)
+ = single crochet (sc)
⊤ = double crochet (dc)

Row 8: Ch 1, *sc between 2 LDC, 11 LDC in next sc; rep from * across, sc between last LDC and tch, turn.

Row 9: Ch 4, LDC in first sc, *ch 4, sc in 6th st of 11-LDC group, ch 4, 2 LDC in next sc; rep from * across, turn.

Row 10: Ch 1, * sc between 2 LDC, 13 LDC in next sc; rep from * across, sc between last LDC and tch.
Fasten off.

BOTTOM TIER

Attached underneath both tiers and beg by working in Top Tier. With WS facing, join yarn to beg of Top Tier Row 2.

Row 1: Sc in first sc; *ch 7, sc around middle of first ch-4 in Row 2 between 4th and 5th dc of Row 3, *ch 7, fpdc (see page 180) around middle sc of next 3-sc group of Row 2; rep from * across to last ch-4 lp, sc around center of ch-4 lp between last two 4-dc groups, ch 7, sc in last sc of Row 2, turn. *8 (10, 12, 14) ch-lps*

Row 2: Ch 1, sc in first st, *skip 3 chs, 7 LDC in next ch, skip 3 chs, sc in next st; rep from * across, turn. *65 (81, 97, 113) sts or 8 (10, 12, 14) fans*

Row 3: Rep Middle Tier Row 3.

Row 4: Rep Middle Tier Row 4.

Row 5: Rep Middle Tier Row 3 .

L and XL Only

Next 2 Rows: Rep Middle Tier Row 4; then Row 3.

All Sizes

Next Row: Rep Middle Tier Row 6.

Next Row: Rep Middle Tier Row 7.

Next 4 (4, 4, 6) Rows: Rep last 2 rows for 2 (2, 2, 3) times.

Next 3 Rows: Rep Middle Tier Rows 8–10. Fasten off.

NECK RUFFLE

Rotate work so Top Tier foundation ch is at top. With RS facing, join yarn to first foundation chain at upper right corner.

Row 1: 2 sc in each st across, turn. *86 (114, 142, 170) hdc*

Row 2: Ch 1, sc across.

Fasten off.

FINISHING

Weave in ends. Steam block all tiers and ruffle to finished measurements, pinning bow ties to lay flat. Sew bead to middle chain at bottom of each bow tie.

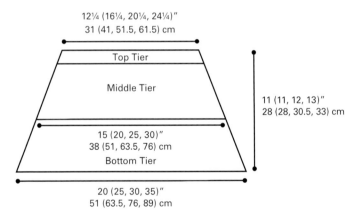

CROCHETED I-CORD

Make 39" (1 m) long crocheted I-cord (see page 196). Weave I-cord through open lps between Top Tier's Rows 1 and 2.

Which two of Jane Austen's novels are partially set in Bath?

Find out on page 203.

DOLL'S CAPELET

Ch 58

Row 1: Sc in 2nd ch from hk, *skip 3 ch, 7 LDC in next ch, skip 3 ch, sc in next ch; rep from * across, turn. *7 fans or 57 sts*

Row 2: Ch 4, LDC in first sc, *ch 2,sc in 4th st of 7-LDC group, ch 2, 2 LDC in next sc; rep from * across, turn.

Row 3: Ch 1, *sc between 2 LDC, 9 LDC in next sc; rep from * across, sc between last LDC and tch, turn.

Row 4: Ch 4, LDC in first sc, *ch 3, sc in 5th st of 9-LDC group, ch 3, 2 LDC in next sc; rep from * across, turn.

Row 5: Ch 1, *sc between 2 LDC, 11 LDC in next sc; rep from * across, sc between last LDC and tch. Fasten off.

NECK RUFFLE

Rotate work so foundation ch is at top. Join yarn to first ch at upper right corner.

Row 1 (gathering row): Ch 1, work 29 sc evenly spaced across, turn.

Row 2: Ch 4 (count as dc and ch 1), skip next sc, dc in next . sc, *ch 1, skip 1 sc, dc in next sc; rep from * across, turn. *15 dc sts*

Row 3: Ch 1, 2 sc in each sc and ch-1 sp across, turn. *58 sts*

Row 4: Ch 1, sc in each st across. Fasten off.

FINISHING

Make enough ch sts for 25" (63.5 cm). Be careful not to stretch chain when measuring. Fasten off. Weave in ends. Thread crocheted ch through (dc, ch 1) row.

CHAPTER 7

The Sitting Room: A Place to Learn the Essentials

"Birth and good manners are essential; but a little

learning is by no means a dangerous thing

in good company; on the contrary, it will do very well."

—*Persuasion*

f you are new to the art of crochet (or if your last project turned out less than desirable), taking the time to study the finer points of crochet construction will serve to increase your accomplishment and your happiness with your end project.

THE STITCHER'S KIT

Known as a "huswife" during the Regency period, a stitcher's kit is simply a bag, workbasket, or box used to keep all needlework tools and accoutrements in good order and close at hand. In each pattern, under materials, is a listing for a Stitcher's Kit. At a minimum, your kit should include crochet hooks of various sizes, stitch markers, a ruler, straight pins, scissors, sewing threads, a beading needle, and a tapestry needle, as well as rust-free T-pins and a surface suitable for blocking. If you do not own these items already, you will want to work toward acquiring them.

GAUGE

When crocheting any design that needs to fit properly, correct gauge is essential—an absolute must. If you do not make up a gauge swatch (a small crocheted sample usually made in the pattern stitch), you are likely to end up with a project that is too large or too small and you run the risk of being short on yarn. Gauge, sometimes also referred to as tension, is simply the number of stitches and rows worked and then counted within a certain area of the crocheted fabric, perhaps per inch (or, typically, 4"/10 cm). Almost all patterns have an entry near the start of the instructions noting the gauge you need to achieve to successfully create the project.

SWATCHING

Your starting point is the Stitch Guide, where you will find (among other delights) the stitch pattern called for in the project's gauge entry. There, the number of beginning chains needed is noted. For example, in An Afternoon at Pemberley (page 12), the gauge is "2 fantails and 8 rows = 4" (10 cm). Under the Stitch Guide, we read the fantail stitch pattern has a foundation chain multiple of 8 + 2. To make the gauge swatch large enough to provide an accurate measurement of gauge, chain a multiple of 8 that will result in a swatch at least 4" (10 cm) wide then chain the additional 2 chain stitches necessary for the foundation chain. Subsequent rows would then be worked according to the stitch pattern given until a minumum of 4" (10 cm) has been reached. To determine if your gauge matches that of the pattern, lay the swatch flat, place a ruler on top and count the number of stitches and rows over an inch (or 4"/10 cm), per the gauge entry. Repeat this measuring two or three times on different areas of the swatch to confirm measurements. Stitches and rows, especially if they are of a smaller nature such as the stitch pattern used in the Summers at Mansfield Park Dress (page 171), need to be counted and recounted in ample lighting. Being off just as little as one stitch in 4" (10 cm) may result in a garment that is one size larger or smaller than expected.

If you have more stitches per inch than the pattern gauge calls for, your stitches are too small and will need to be made bigger by switching to a larger hook. If you have too few stitches, you need to produce more stitches in 1" (2.5 cm) by using a smaller hook. Make sure you work another gauge swatch with the new hook size. Continue swatching and revising the hook size until the stitches and rows per inch (or 4"/10 cm) equal those of the pattern gauge. Whatever size hook this results in is the size hook you should use regardless of the size the pattern suggests. Note: In addition to video tutorials on all the stitch patterns used in this book, a video tutorial on swatching to gauge can be found at the website www.stitch scene.com.

HUNG GAUGE

Hung gauge, in its simplest explanation, refers to a gauge swatch that is not measured flat but rather measured after the swatch has hung vertically, as it would on your body. Some yarn fibers, most famously cotton, stretch out and do not return to their original shape. First hang the swatch vertically with clothespins attached to the bottom edge to add weight (to mimic gravity or the weight of additional yarn). After allowing the gauge swatch to hang a day or two, measure the stitches and rows to determine if the correct gauge has been achieved. You chance your happiness with the end result if you begin your project without determining your correct hook size by making an accurate gauge swatch.

FIT

Second only to gauge in importance when stitching a garment is choosing the best pattern size for your body. It is essential to follow a few guidelines.

MEASURE YOURSELF

When making a sweater, wrap the tape measure around your body at the fullest part of your bust. When measuring for a skirt, the most important number is the circumference at the fullest part of your lower body. For most people this is the hips, but it could be your belly or even the top of your thighs.

CHECK THE FINISHED SIZES

Every garment pattern in this book has this entry. There could be only one number, or it may be followed by one or more additional numbers in parentheses, with each number representing a different garment size. Let us examine the Becoming Jane Sweater (page 41). Under the pattern's Finished Size heading it reads Size XS (S, M, L, 1X, 2X) to fit finished bust circumference of 33¼ (36, 40, 42½, 45¼, 50½)"/84.5 (91.5, 101.5, 108, 115, 128.5) cm.

From this we learn that the finished bust circumference of the size Medium will be 40"/101.5 cm. Do not make the mistake of choosing your garment size by simply using the entry that is nearest to your body measurement. First consider ease.

CONSIDER THE EASE

Ease is the difference between your body measurement and

what the garment measures in that same area. Look at the way the garment fits the model in the project photo. Is it snug? Then it is very close-fitting and has minimal ease. If the garment hangs loosely, then it was designed to be oversized, or have plenty (6"/15 cm or more) of ease.

Looking again at the Becoming Jane Sweater (page 41) as an example, if your bust measures 34" (86.5 cm) and you wish to have a standard fitting sweater as shown in the photo on page 40, select the size that produces the 36" (91.5 cm). Choose the 33½" (85 cm) size only if you want the garment to be a very close fit and, alternatively, the 40" (101.5 cm) if you prefer a very roomy sweater. The Craft Yarn Council (www.craftyarncouncil.com) suggests the following for fit:

- Very-close fitting: Actual chest/bust measurement or less
- Close-fitting: 1–2"/2.5-5 cm
- Standard-fitting: 2–4"/5–10 cm
- Loose-fitting: 4–6"/10–15 cm
- Oversized: 6"/15 cm or more

LOOK AT THE SCHEMATICS

Next, because every body is different, study the pattern's schematics. These illustrations show the shape of the primary garment pieces before assembly, with finished dimensions indicated for all sizes to help you identify what adjustments may need to be made. You may require the torso or sleeve measurement to be longer or shorter than given in the schematic for the size you selected.

THINK ABOUT THE FABRIC

If you are uncertain as to which size you should choose, remember most crocheted fabric has give. You can always block (see page 195) a piece slightly larger than noted in the finished measurements and schematics, but unless felting, you can't go smaller.

SKILL LEVELS

Each pattern in this book features an icon denoting the pattern's scale of difficulty as detailed here.

Perfect for those who have not yet had their come-out. Your first season is just around the corner. Only a short time more is needed in the school room before you master the basic stitches. But who minds with that fine English tutor you can dream of?

Invitation to Almacks? Check. You have had your crochet debut and are comfortable with hook in hand. Finishing school has prepared you for the simple shaping and seaming techniques required in these patterns.

For those who are well established in society. You dance gracefully and effortlessly through your days, managing your household with ease, being all that is charitable and stitching up whatever you enjoy. You may be the more experienced stitcher but you are by no means "on the shelf."

BASIC STITCHES

Following are the basic techniques for making crocheted stitches. In crochet, most stitches are variations of one of these beginning stitches. In learning these stitches, you will find them to be progressive—that is, in most cases each stitch builds upon the previous one to create a new stitch with the addition of one more simple step. A video stitch tutorial of each of the following stitches as well as every stitch used in each pattern of this book can be found at www.stitchscene.com/tutorials.

SLIP KNOT

Most crochet begins with a slip knot as it is a simple way to place the first working loop on the hook.

1. Leaving at least 6" (15 cm) of yarn tail (end) in left hand, create a loop by taking the yarn attached to the ball with your right hand and then winding it over the top of your fingers holding the yarn tail. This forms a loop. Let working yarn (the yarn attached to the ball) fall behind the loop.
2. With hook, draw through lp. Pull yarn tail in left hand away from hook to tighten loop.

A. Wrap yarn around fingers allowing working end to fall behind loop.

B. With hook, reach through loop, catch the yarn's working end and draw through loop.

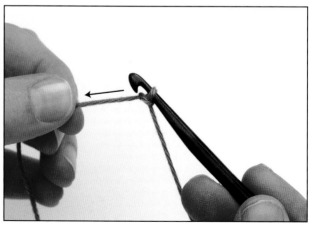

C. Tighen knot by gently pulling yarn tail in direction of arrow.

CHAIN STITCH (ch)

The chain stitch is often used for the beginning or foundation chain of many crochet patterns. However, it can also be used in any number within a stitch pattern to create open spaces. When creating the chain stitch for the beginning chain, continue making chain stitches until the specific number, as stated in the pattern, is reached. Do not include the slip knot in this count. See page 187 for guidance on the number of chain stitches to make if working a gauge swatch.

1. Holding working yarn in your left hand and hook in your right, bring hook under yarn so yarn is positioned from back to front over hook's shaft (figure D) This is referred to as a yarn over (yo). This yarn over is used over and over again in crochet and should also be worked in a consistent manner with yarn positioned from back to front over the hook.

2. Grab working yarn in crook of hook and draw through loop (the slip knot) located on hook (figure E). One loop remains on hook. You have made one chain. Ignore the slip knot for the rest of your stitching because it doesn't "count" as a stitch.

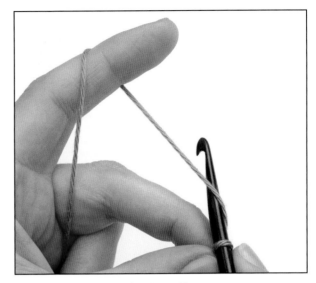

D. Yarn over by placing hook under working yarn.

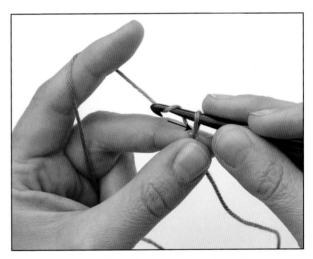

E. After yarn over, catch yarn in hook and draw through loop on hook—1 chain stitch made.

SLIP STITCH (sl st)

1. With one loop already on hook (on occasion there may be more than one stitch or loop already on hook), insert hook into stitch (or position hook into crocheted fabric, also referred to as work) as directed.

2. Wrap yarn over hook and draw yarn through stitch (or work) and loop already on hook (figure F). A slip stitch always draws through everything that is on the hook. Upon completion one loop remains on hook.

F. Insert hook into top of stitch (the two strands that form a V or teardrop shape), yarn over and draw through all loops on hook—slip stitch made.

SINGLE CROCHET STITCH (sc)

1. Insert hook into stitch (or position it in the work) as directed.

2. Wrap yarn over hook and draw through stitch (or work) already on hook (figure G). There are now two loops on the hook.

3. Wrap yarn over hook and draw through both loops on hook (figure H). One loop remains on the hook.

G. Insert hook into top of stitch yarn over and draw yarn through stitch loops only.

H. Yarn over and draw through remaining two loops on hook—a single crochet stitch made.

HALF DOUBLE CROCHET (hdc)

1. Wrap yarn over hook and insert hook into stitch (or position it in the work as directed).

2. Wrap yarn over hook and draw through the stitch (or work) already on hook (figure I). There are now three loops on the hook.

3. Wrap yarn over hook and draw through all three loops on the hook (figure J). One loop remains on the hook.

I. Yarn over, then insert hook into stitch, draw yarn through stitch loops only.

J. Yarn over and draw yarn through remaining three loops on hook— one half double crochet stitch made.

DOUBLE CROCHET STITCH (dc)

The double crochet stitches shown in the pictures on page 194 are worked loosely for visual clarity. Yours will be worked much more closely together.

1. Wrap yarn over hook and insert hook into stitch (or position it in the work) as directed.

2. Wrap yarn over hook and draw through stitch (or work) already on the hook (figure K). There are now three loops on the hook.

3. Wrap yarn over hook and draw through two of the loops already on hook (figure L). There are now two loops on the hook.

4. Wrap yarn over and draw through remaining two loops on hook (figure M). One loop remains on the hook.

K. Yarn over, insert hook into stitch and draw through loops of stitch only.

M. Yarn over and draw through last two loops on hook—one double crochet stitch made.

L. Yarn over and draw through first two loops.

BACK/FRONT LOOP ONLY (blo/flo)

Work as for stitch given EXCEPT insert hook under only one of the top two loops of the stitch: Insert hook under loop nearest to you to work in the front loop only (flo) of the stitch. Insert hook under the loop farthest away from you to work in the back loop only (blo) of the stitch.

FASTENING OFF

Once the last stitch has been worked, the work must be fastened off. To fasten off, simply cut the working yarn at a minimum of 6" (15 cm) from work. Draw yarn end through loop on hook. Pull tight. With yarn or tapestry needle, weave in the yarn end, being careful not to split yarn and ensuring it does not show on the right side of the fabric.

SPECIAL TECHNIQUES

Throughout this book, a number of techniques are used in creating some of the designs. Detailed procedures for each technique are written below and a video stitch tutorial of each can be viewed at www.stitchscene.com/tutorials.

BLOCKING

Don't think of blocking as a superfluous extra step—rather, it is the step that gives your project that something extra. Many fibers require different methods of blocking so it is best to use the suggested method of blocking given in the Finishing section of each pattern in this book. If substituting yarn from that given in the materials, refer to the yarn's wrapper or manufacturer's website for the recommended method of blocking.

If projects are made in pieces they are usually blocked prior to seaming. Projects worked in the round (joined at the end of every row) are blocked later. The point at which an item should be blocked is noted for every project in this book.

STEAM BLOCKING

Steam blocking is a gentler way to relax and set fibers. Place piece flat on a blocking board, or carpeted floor lined with several dry towels. Pin piece to dimensions noted on pattern's schematic. Holding a fabric steamer or iron with a high steam setting just above piece, steam. Be sure not to touch crocheted fabric as contact may damage yarn fibers. Let dry completely.

SPRITZ BLOCKING

Misting a garment lightly with water is another way to gently relax and set yarn fibers. Place piece flat on a blocking board, or carpeted floor lined with several dry towels. Pin piece to dimensions noted on schematic then mist with water until it is thoroughly damp but not soaking wet. Let dry completely.

WET BLOCKING

This process allows for greatest stretch of finished work. To wet block, gently place crocheted fabric in tepid water. Softly press fabric under water to completely submerge. Do not agitate. Let soak for at least twenty minutes to ensure all of the fibers absorb water. Lift crocheted fabric out of water and gently press water out of fabric. Never wring crocheted fabric as some fibers are very fragile when wet. Roll work in towels to absorb even more water, and let sit for several minutes. Place piece flat on a blocking board, or carpeted floor lined with several dry towels. Pin crocheted piece to dimensions noted on schematics. Let dry completely (this may take several days).

CHANGING COLORS

When changing colors, work the specified stitch until it is almost complete with only the last two loops remaining on the hook. Yarn over hook with new color and draw through all of the loops on hook to complete stitch. If directed, fasten off first color leaving at least 6" (15 cm) tail for weaving in. Continue stitching with new color.

CROCHETED I-CORD

With slip knot on hook, ch 3, turn.

Row 1: Working in back loop only, insert hook in 2nd ch from hook, yo and draw through lp, insert hook in back loop only of 3rd ch from hook, yo and draw through a lp – 3 lps on hook.

Row 2: Remove the last two loops from hook holding them securely with hand, yo, draw through loop on hook, place middle loop held in other hand onto hook, yo and draw through this middle lp, place last loop held in other hand onto hook, yo and draw through this end lp. Do not turn.

Repeat row 2 until the desired length of crocheted cord has been reached.

CROCHET CASING STITCH

1. Pin the elastic to the wrong side of garment.
2. With a small hook and a crochet thread that matches garment, form slip knot on hook.
3. To join yarn to fabric, sl st to crocheted fabric on left side of elastic.
4. Work enough chains to cross over elastic.
5. Sl st to right side of elastic.
6. Continue to form a zigzag chain that fits snugly over the elastic anchored to the garment with slip stitches at each zigzag point.

ELASTIC WAIST CASING

An elastic waist is simple to achieve.

1. Working at waistline, fold the crocheted fabric to the wrong side.
2. Using yarn from project, whipstitch folded edge to wrong side of fabric leaving a 3" (7.5 cm) opening for inserting elastic.
3. Cut elastic equal to your waist measurement plus 1" (2.5 cm). Place a safety pin in one end of the elastic.
4. Use the safety pin to draw the elastic through the opening in the waistband, all the way around the waistband, being careful not to lose the opposite end of the elastic.
5. Once the elastic is pulled through waist casing, pin edges of elastic together. Try on to ensure this is a comfortable fit.
6. Overlap the elastic, then using sewing thread, machine or hand stitch the elastic together.
7. Using yarn from project, whipstitch the opening of the waistband closed.

FELTING

Though the term is actually *fulling*, it is identified as felting by the majority of stitchers. It is the process of melding stitches together through the use of hot water and agitation. Though felting can be done by agitating the piece by hand, a washing machine set to the hot/cold water cycle and on the smallest load cycle will do the job quickly and nicely.

1. Place a small amount of detergent in hot water then add the piece to be felted.
2. Let the machine continue agitating until the desired amount of felting (determined by size and stitch definition, or lack thereof) is achieved. When first checking the crocheted piece it may appear larger rather than smaller. This is normal as the stitches will relax before they begin to tighten.
3. Once felting is as desired, let the machine drain. Achieving the desired level of felting may take several runs through the agitation cycle.
4. Rinse the project with cool water and then roll in a towel to absorb excess water.
5. Shape or block as pattern requires, then let dry.
6. Neatly finish by brushing felted project with sweater comb. Use scissors to snip off any loose fuzzy tidbits off surface.

HAIRPIN LACE

Set hairpin lace loom to width noted in pattern.

1. Slide slip knot onto the left prong of the loom and center it between the two prongs. Yarn tails should remain in front of loom.
2. Wrap yarn from front to back over the right side prong. Working yarn is now at the back of the loom. Yarn should be held across the back of the loom.
3. Insert hook into lengthened slip knot. Yo and draw through loop on hook, then ch 1.
4. Keeping the loop on hook, twist hook upside down so handle is near the top of loom rather than the bottom.
5. Being sure to keep yarn at the back of the loom, flip loom by bringing the right prong toward you. The right prong now becomes the left prong.
6. Return hook to working hold and insert hook under topmost loop on left prong. Two loops are now on hook, work one sc. Be sure to keep single crochet stitch centered between prongs.

Repeat steps 4–6 until the number of loops as determined by pattern have been achieved.

Creating hairpin lace for the first time requires some practice. Join me in my sitting room at www.stitchscene.com for a video tutorial on how to make hairpin lace.

MONK'S CORD

Shorter lengths are easier to work with until you grasp the instructions, so make a practice cord using shorter lengths of yarn.

1. Measure 4 strands of yarn, each five times as long as desired finished cord. Should you decide your swatch cord to be thicker than you like, decrease to 3 strands.
2. Holding strands together, tie a knot tightly on one end leaving a 6" (15 cm) tail. Secure knot to an object or have a friend hold this end.
3. Next, move backward until yarn is stretched out to its full length. Begin twisting cord. Direction of twist does not matter as long as direction remains consistent.
4. Keep twisting until yarn becomes difficult to twist.
5. Maintaining a firm hold on the yarn, walk forward. If rope begins to kink and twist back on itself you have twisted enough. (If it doesn't, step back and keep twisting).
6. Still gripping your end tightly, grab the opposite end of the cord firmly. Move one cord to the other hand so you are holding both ends in one hand and the cord is folded in half. Carefully knot the ends together. Relax grip and allow both cords to twist together as one. Run hand down length of cord smoothing into a neat twist. Knot the other end at desired length. Trim ends.

SEAMING

Many methods of seaming exist and it is recommended to use the method that most appeals to you unless a pattern notes otherwise, usually for decorative purposes. Instructions for common seaming methods are listed here.

MATTRESS STITCH

Used mostly for joining vertical edges, this form of seaming is worked on the right side of the crocheted fabric. This technique creates an almost invisible seam where the selvedges created by the seaming roll toward each other on the wrong side of fabric.

1. Thread tapestry needle with yarn tail or a long section of yarn.
2. With right sides of both pieces of work facing you, butt together the edges that will be seamed and align rows. Now insert needle tip down into fabric on right side of seam and up through the fabric (still on right side of seam) picking up a stitch.
3. Next, bring the needle to the left side of seam and insert needle into corresponding location as on right side.
4. Insert needle tip down into fabric and then up through fabric (still on left side of seam) to pick up a stitch. Pull yarn to bring seams together.
5. Continue to work along the seam, picking up a stitch from the right side and then the left side, pulling the needle and yarn as each stitch is worked to tighten seam.

BACK STITCH

This seam works well for uneven edges or when the size of the garment needs altering.

1. Thread tapestry needle with yarn. With right sides of crocheted fabric facing each other and edges to be seamed facing upward, insert needle from front to back through the corresponding stitches on each piece, taking care not to split yarn. Draw yarn through to back.
2. Skip one stitch, insert needle from back to front in next stitch and draw yarn through to front.
3. Insert needle from front to back in skipped stitch and draw yarn through to back.

Repeat steps 2 and 3 along length of the seam.

SLIP STITCH

This type of seam creates a firm stitch with little stretch.

1. Begin with slip knot on hook (see page 190), and right sides of crocheted pieces facing each other. Edges to be seamed should be facing upward.
2. Insert hook through corresponding stitches on edges of each piece beings seamed.
3. Yo, draw yarn through both crocheted pieces and draw through lp on hook.

Repeat steps 2 and 3 along length of the seam.

WHIPSTITCH

Most often worked on the inside of a garment, place right sides of the two pieces to be seamed together with edges to be seamed facing upward. When beginning this stitch, work several stitches over your yarn tail to secure and hide the yarn end.

1. Working along the top edge to be seamed, bring threaded needle through the two edges from back to front.
2. Bring yarn over the edge and insert threaded needle from back to front again. Continue along seam in this manner.

INTERNATIONAL CROCHET TERM TRANSLATION

AMERICAN	INTERNATIONAL
slip stitch (sl st)	single crochet (sc)
single crochet (sc)	double crochet (dc)
half double crochet (hdc)	half treble crochet (htr)
double crochet (dc)	treble crochet (tr)
treble crochet (tr)	double treble crochet (dtr)
double treble crochet (dtr)	triple treble crochet (ttr)
skip	miss

STANDARD AMERICAN CROCHET ABBREVIATIONS

1x 1 extra large	**hdc2tog** half double crochet 2 stitches together	**sc** single crochet stitch(es)
2x 2 extra large	**inc** increase(s)(ing)	**sc2tog** single crochet two stitches together
beg begin(ning)	**L** large	**sl st** slip stitch(s)
blo back loop only	**lp(s)** loop(s)	**sk** skip
CC coordinating color	**m** meter(s)	**sp(s)** space(s)
ch(s) chain(s)	**MC** main color	**ssc** split single crochet stitch(es)
cm centimeter(s)	**M** medium	**st(s)** stitch(es)
col color(s)	**mm** millimeter(s)	**tch** turning chain(s)
cont continue(s)(ing)	**oz** ounce(s)	**tog** together
dc double crochet stitch(es)	**patt** pattern(s)	**tr** treble stitch(es)
dec decrease(s)(ing)	**pm** place marker	**tsp** teaspoon(s)
flo front loop only	**RS** right side(s)	**WS** wrong side(s)
foll follow(s)(ing)	**Rem** remain(s)(ing)	**XS** extra small
fpdc front post double crochet stitch(es)	**rep** repeat(s)(ing)	**yd(s)** yard(s)
fpsc front post single crochet stitch(es)	**rev sc** reverse single crochet stitch(es)	**yo** wrap yarn over hook
fsc foundation single crochet stitch(es)	**rnd(s)** round(s)	
hdc half double crochet stitch(es)	**S** small	

SOURCES FOR FURTHER READING

The Craft Yarn Council has excellent information on how to read crochet patterns and stitch charts. Visit http://www.craftyarn council.com/tip_crochet.html

BIBLIOGRAPHY

Austen-Leigh, James-Edward. *A Memoir of Jane Austen* (1870). Oxford University Press, 1926.

Byrde, Penelope. *Jane Austen Fashion: Fashion and Needlework in the Works of Jane Austen.* Ludlow: Moonrise, 2008.

Ross, Josephine. *Jane Austen: a Companion.* New Brunswick, NJ: Rutgers UP, 2003.

RESOURCES

Thank you to the following suppliers of yarn, notions, and accessories used throughout this book. Your generous support is greatly appreciated!

YARN

Bernat

(888) 368-8401

320 Livingstone Ave. S.

Listowel, ON

Canada N4W 3H3

bernat.com

• *Bernat Alpaca*

Berroco Inc.

(508) 278-2527

PO Box 367

14 Elmdale Road

Uxbridge, MA 01569

berroco.com

• *Comfort*

• *Vintage*

Brown Sheep Company

(800) 826-9136

100662 County Road 16

Mitchell, NE 69357

brownsheep.com

• *Burley Spun*

Caron International

PO Box 222

Washington, NC 27889

naturallycaron.com

• *Spa*

Cascade Yarns

(206) 574-0440

1224 Andover Park E

Tukwila, WA 98188

cascadeyarns.com

• *Heritage*

• *Ultra Pima*

• *Venezia Worsted*

Classic Elite Yarns

(978) 453-2837

122 Western Avenue

Lowell, MA 01851-1434

classiceliteyarns.com

• *Moorland*

Coats & Clark

(800) 648-1479

Consumer Services

PO Box 12229

Greenville, SC 29612-0029

coatsandclark.com

• *Aunt Lydia's Bamboo Crochet Thread*

• *Aunt Lydia's Classic Crochet Thread*

• *J&P Coats Royale Fashion Thread*

DMC

(800) 275-4117

10 Basin Drive, Suite 130

Kearny, NJ 07032

dmc.com

• *Senso Microfiber Cotton*

• *Linen Floss*

Knit Picks

(800) 574-1323

13118 NE 4th Street

Vancouver, WA 98684

knitpicks.com

• *City Tweed DK*

• *CotLin DK*

• *Gloss*

Lion Brand Yarn

(800) 258-9276

135 Kero Road

Carlstadt, NJ 07072

lionbrand.com

• *Moonlight Mohair*

Patons Yarn

(888) 368-8401

320 Livingstone Ave. S.

Listowel, ON

Canada N4W 3H3

patonsyarns.com

• *Patons Décor*

• *Patons Classic Wool*

Plymouth Yarn

Company Inc.

(215) 788-0459

PO Box 28

Bristol, PA 19007

plymouthyarn.com

• *Alpaca Boucle*

Tilli Tomas

(617)524-3330

tillitomas.com

• *Voile de la Mer*

Westminster Fibers Inc

(800) 445-9276

165 Ledge Street

Nashua, NH 03060

Westminsterfibers.com

• *Rowan Kid Classic*

• *Rowan Siena*

• *Rowan Silky Tweed*

• *Nashua Daylily*

• *Nashua Julia*

• *Kertzer Northern Worsted*

Universal Yarn

(877) 864-9276

284 Ann Street

Concord, NC 28025

universalyarn.com

• *Fibra Natura Flax*

BUTTONS

Blumenthal Lansing

Company

(800) 553-4158

1929 Main Street

Lansing, IA 52151

blumenthallansing.com

• *La Mode Buttons*

Dill Buttons of America Inc.

(888) 460-7555

50 Choate Circle

Montoursville, PA 17754

dill-buttons.com

• *Dill Buttons*

ACCOMPANYING CLOTHING, ACCESSORIES, AND PROPS

Victorian Trading Company

(913)438-3995

15600 West 99th Street

Lenexa, KS 66219

victoriantradingco.com

PHOTOGRAPHY

Chris Hynes Photography

(312) 775-2551

931 E Main Street #3

Madison, WI 53703

chrishynesphoto.com

JEWELRY

Leda Rawlins Designs

PO Box 5015

Madison, WI 53705

ledarawlins.com

INDOOR LOCATION

Mansion Hill Inn

(800) 798-9070

424 N Pinckney Street

Madison, WI 53703

mansionhillinn.com

TRIVIA AND QUIZ ANSWERS

SENSE OR SENSIBILITY— WHICH SISTER ARE YOU?
(page 62)

1. One point if you answered a, two points for b, three points for c.
2. One point if you answered yes, two points for no.
3. One point if you answered a, two points for b, 3 points for c.
4. One point if you answered yes, two points for no.
5. Zero points if you answered yes, two points for a no.
6. One point if you answered yes, two points for no.
7. One point if you answered no, three points if you answered yes.

6–9 points: Hard to get, whatever for? You wear your heart on sleeve . . . and your face, your hand, your leg. Anywhere and anyway you can display your love, dear Marianne, you do so proudly.

10–13 points: The best of both sisters, you let a man know when you are interested without being too forward. After all, you understand he places a greater value on that which is more difficult to obtain.

14–17 points: Like Elinor, you run the risk of his not being aware of your interest. A discerning man will be aware of your qualities, yet men like that can be hard to find.

LETTERS (page 75)

1. C
2. D
3. B
4. C

WHICH CHARACTERS SAID THESE SWOON-WORTHY LINES?
(page 91)

1. Edward Ferrar
2. Captain Wentworth
3. Willoughby
4. Mr. Darcy
5. Mr. Collins
6. Captain Wentworth
7. Mr. Elton
8. John Thorpe
9. Frank Churchill
10. Captain Wentworth
11. Willoughby
12. Mr. Knightley
13. Mr. Darcy

HARRIET SMITH (page 94)

3 men: Mr. Martin, Mr. Elton, Mr. Knightley (4 if you counted Emma's assumption that Harriet likes Mr. Churchill.

MR. BINGLEY'S SISTERS (page 96)

5 and 2

WHICH TWO SISTERS MARRIED THE SAME DAY? (page 146)

Elizabeth and Jane Bennet

YOUNG CHILD QUIZ (page 163)

1. Margaret
2. Susan
3. Emma

NOVELS PARTIALLY SET IN BATH
(page 184)

1. *Northanger Abbey*
2. *Persuasion*

ART CREDITS

On the front cover and p. 8: *Jane Austen*, engraving published in *Little Journeys to the Homes of Famous Women*, 1897. Private Collection/ Ken Welsh/The Bridgeman Art Library

p. 6: *Hide-and-Seek*, illustration from *Le Bon Genre*, French School, early 19th century. Bibliotheque des Arts Decoratifs, Paris, France/ Archives Charmet/The Bridgeman Art Library

p. 9: *Jane Austen*, by Ozias Humphry, ca. 1792–93. Private Collection/ The Bridgeman Art Library

p. 10: *Mrs. John Hazlitt Reading* by John Hazlitt, 19th century. ©Maidstone Museum and Art Gallery, Kent, UK/The Bridgeman Art Library

p. 21: *Portrait of a Lady* by Henry Edridge, 1806. ©Bolton Museum and Art Gallery, Lancashire, UK/The Bridgeman Art Library

p. 31: *Jane Austen*, English School, 18th century. Private Collection/ The Bridgeman Art Library

p. 45: *In Love* by Marcus Stone (1840–1921). Nottingham City Museums and Galleries (Nottingham Castle)/The Bridgeman Art Library

p. 50: Designs for Regency Hats, 1828. Private Collection/© Charles Plante Fine Arts/The Bridgeman Art Library

p. 54: *Chawton House and Church*, English School, 1809. Chawton House, Hampshire, UK/The Bridgeman Art Library

p. 62: *Two Women Reading in an Interior* by Jean Georges Ferry, 19th century. Private Collection/©Gavin Graham Gallery, London, UK/The Bridgeman Art Library

p. 75: *In the Library, St. James' Square*, attributed to Thomas Pole, ca.1805–06. ©Bristol City Museum and Art Gallery, UK/The Bridgeman Art Library

p. 76: *Courtship* by George Goodwin Kilburne (1839–1924). Private Collection/The Bridgeman Art Library

p. 91: *The Kiss* by G. Baldry, 19th century. Simon Carter Gallery, Woodbridge, Suffolk, UK/The Bridgeman Art Library

p. 94: Silhouette of Cassandra Austen by John Meiers, ca.1809. Private Collection/The Bridgeman Art Library

p. 96: *Portrait of Captain and Mrs. George Ruddle* by Richard Dighton, ca.1835. ©Cheltenham Art Gallery & Museums, Gloucestershire, UK/The Bridgeman Art Library

p. 101: *Promenade* by Constant-Emile Troyon (1810–65). Private Collection/Courtesy of Thomas Brod and Patrick Pilkington/ The Bridgeman Art Library

p. 105: *Anticipation* by James W. Usher, 1916. Lincolnshire County Council, Usher Gallery, Lincoln, UK/The Bridgeman Art Library

p. 108: *Walking Dresses*, fashion plate from *Ackermann's Repository of Arts*, published 1st June 1809. Private Collection/The Stapleton Collection/The Bridgeman Art Library

p. 112: *The Sisters* by James W. Usher (1845–1921). Lincolnshire County Council, Usher Gallery, Lincoln, UK/The Bridgeman Art Library

p. 119: *A Woman and Her Beau Spinning Thread* by Isabella Downman, 18th century. Private Collection/Abbott and Holder, London, UK/ The Bridgeman Art Library

p. 129: *Spinning, Reading and Writing, 17th February 1807* by John Harden. ©Abbot Hall Art Gallery, Kendal, Cumbria, UK/The Bridgeman Art Library

p. 130: *An Introduction: Gay moments of Logic, Jerry, Tom and Corinthian Kate*, from *Life in London* by Pierce Egan, 1821, aquatint by I. Robert & George Cruikshank. Private Collection/The Stapleton Collection/The Bridgeman Art Library

p. 144: *Lady Sewing* by William Henry Hunt, ca.1830. Manchester Art Gallery, UK/The Bridgeman Art Library

p. 146: *Summer Fashions for 1836*, English School. Westminster Library, London/The Bridgeman Art Library

p. 151: *Parisian ball dress*, published in *Ackermann's Repository for Arts*, April 1817. Fashion Museum, Bath and North East Somerset Council/The Bridgeman Art Library

p. 155: *An Elegant Lady* by Constantin Guys, (1802–92). Private Collection/Photo ©Peter Nahum at The Leicester Galleries, London/ The Bridgeman Art Library

p. 159: *A Child* by Edward Bird (1772–1819). ©Wolverhampton Art Gallery, West Midlands, UK/The Bridgeman Art Library

p. 163: *The Lesson* by William Frederick Witherington (1785–1865). ©Wolverhampton Art Gallery, West Midlands, UK/The Bridgeman Art Library

p. 172: *Parisian evening dress*, published in *La Belle Assemblée*, May 1817. Fashion Museum, Bath and North East Somerset Council/ The Bridgeman Art Library

p. 188: *Charles Moran and his wife Jane Bodin with Jane and William, 1812* by Adam Buck. Private Collection/The Bridgeman Art Library

INDEX

✺ ACKNOWLEDGMENTS ✺

Though no woman is an island, I certainly try to be; but not for the work of several talented and creative women this book would not exist. A special shout out to Kate Epstein, a most agreeable and helpful agent. Thank you to my editor Cindy De La Hoz, who caught the vision for this book and ran with it. To Susan Huxley—a thank you is simply not enough for going the extra mile to allow me to learn from your expertise as we went along. To Chris H., Amy R, my mother Terri, and sister Jessica, all who so graciously gave of their time and creative spirit—you are the best! Thank you to Dora O. for the time, insight, and encouragement you have given through mentoring. And to my friends and family, too numerous to name, yet important to acknowledge for the constructive feedback given when asked, and for sharing photo props I spied in your home. My heartfelt gratitude to my husband Lance, and my children, Nathan and Anna, for both the encouragement and support given, especially when the process grew long and you were counting the days until the end. Most importantly, thank you to my Heavenly Father—all that is good within me comes from Him.